Black, Brown, and White
on the Border

Black, Brown, and White on the Border

Marc Zimmerman

LACASA
CHICAGO
Latin American/Latin@ Cultural
Activities and Studies Arena

Zimmerman, Marc. 1939.

ISBN Paperback: 978-1-961472-05-1
ISBN Hardcover: 978-1-961472-06-8
Preassigned Control Number (PCN): 9781960399373
Library of Congress Control Number (LCC): 2023905369

Listed in the Catalogue of the Library of Congress:

1. Fiction 2. Auto Fiction 3. Mexico/ Mexicans 4. African Americans 5. U.S. /Latin America 6. Chicanos. 7. Latinos. 8. Jewish and Italian Americans

LACASA Chicago Books
2120 W. Concord Place
Chicago, IL 60647
Mzimmerman1939@gmail.com Tel 281-513-9475.

www.marczimmerman.net.

"Zimmerman shows us how nothing is more movable than borders, no matter how many fences and walls you build to make them permanent. How borders are ethnic and ethical, geographical, historical, and very, very personal, how we can be here but not there, that we can be this but not that. But do they succeed? Wherever we look, there is always a border—before or behind us or cutting us in two. We're all divided territories, dreaming of what we were, but sensing what our border-crossings have made of us. This book tells us all this and more." **Alessandro Carrera**, Ph.D. & John and Rebecca Moores Professor World Cultures and Literatures, MCL, U. of Houston. Author of *The Voice of Bob Dylan* and *The Color of Dark*.

"Personal and easy to read, with touches of humor, but elegant in his words and thoughts, by a writer who knows the culture and language of the border. The book offers us many perspectives, approaches, and projections... especially on gender... through wonderfully imaginative and truthful stories." **Marta E. Sánchez**, Professor Emerita, U. of *California, San Diego and Arizona U. Author of Chicana Poetry* and *Shakin' Up Race and Gender: Intercultural Connections in Puerto Rican, African American, and Chicano Narratives and Culture.*

"Zimmerman's long involvement with Latino and Latin American concerns has given him many stories to tell. His book captures the the melancholic, magical moments that borders create." **Carolina Rivera Escamilla**, Los Angeles/Salvadoran author of *...after...* and *In a Corner of Your Country.*

For all the others living or gone on one side or another of the border:

Willie Green, Albert Hall, Manzo Hill, Roland McFarland, Floyd Richardson,

Jacqueline and Bill Tunberg, Karl Alexander,

Petra, Victoria, Phyllis, Carolyn, Ernestine,

Carlos Eduarte, Adrienne and Joanne Brown,
And all theirs and many others in Nicaragua and Southern California.

—To all those who struggle as they live on and cross borders, only to fear that they will not be able to ..., or will have to.

—To John Beverley, Alessandro Carrera, Dick Goldberg, Ángel Quintero Rivera, and Samuel Soler and for their support of my post-academic turn toward and certainly not against literature.

—Also to Mario García and Arturo Madrid;

Roberto Márquez, Carolina Rivera and Marta and Rosaura Sánchez.

And of course, to Esther (y su tribu).

Above all, to the memory of my sister, Elaine Brown,

and my friend, José Gamaliel González

Table of Contents

Introduction

1. The Diana Bar

On one of my return visits to Tijuana in the late 1990s, Professor José Manuel Valenzuela Arce told me that he and friends he'd grown up with in the town of Tecate were collaborating on a book of fiction set in the Diana Bar, a small cantina off the central plaza. I told him I'd sometimes visited the bar on my trips to Tecate during my California years.

"Great," he said, amused and surprised. "Why don't you write a story for our book?"

I was very grateful for the offer to be the guest gringo in a Mexican border collection—I took it as a great compliment, but somehow it didn't happen. I tried several times, but I couldn't seem to write that story.

A couple of years later, I visited with José Manuel again, this time with my wife, Esther, and he handed me a small book. "Remember that collection I told you about? . . . Here it is. We wanted your story, but we couldn't wait."

"I'm sorry," I told him, "I just couldn't write it."

"That's because the border cannot be represented," he quipped—though I couldn't tell if he was expressing or parodying faddish border babble.

I looked at the book and was deeply moved, especially since most of the writers, like José Manuel himself, were children of the Tecate Cervecería—children whose parents' hard work at the brewery had provided the basis for them to become professionals and write books like the one in my hand. But something disturbed me all too much. Because the image on the cover was of a very exotic, tropical-looking cantina, famed by two palm trees and the moon above—a dream cantina not much like the Diana of my memory.

"Look," I told my wife, "we have to go to Tecate and see this place!"

So off we went in the late afternoon to Tecate, arriving before dark, driving past the brewery, circling the town plaza so near the brewery and ever so close to the border, until we were in front of the Diana. There it was in its non-splendor: needing a coat of paint, needing all kinds of loving care it was not receiving; not a hint at day's end that the moon would appear—even less of a hint that the palms would appear to frame the saloon.

"Esther," I said, handing her the book, "why don't you stand in front of the bar, and hold up the book while I take your photo?"

Getting down from the car, she stood in front of the bar entrance, and I set up for my photo opportunity: the bar and its presentation on the book cover. I took the shot and then it grew dark.

As we drove back across the border, I remember thinking, what a great image to use for a paper I wanted to write about my crossings. The moon never came out that night.

A few days later, at a Chicago Walgreen's, I saw the developed picture and realized that somehow things had gone wrong. First, the flash had hardly illuminated a thing, and besides for some reason, we could only see part of the façade and one eye and part of the forehead of my wife!

Sometime later, I told José Manuel what had happened.

"I guess that's what I get for using my wife," I offered.

"Tal vez," he answered. "But that's the perfect story for our book about the Diana."

"Yes," I answered, "but I could only write it when the book was published."

"That's the way it is with border stories sometimes," he said. "They don't get told or are told too late, and they come out skewed."

But that wasn't the full story even yet.

"I wanted to capture how your group romanticized the border," I confessed.

"Well, maybe you got it after all. You know," he joined me in this confessional moment (but was he telling the truth?), "I've never been in that bar, and I don't think my friends have either."

It was only some years after I wrote down all this that I fully realized that I'd finally written the border story José Manuel had urged me to write. But the story could only emerge as a result of its not being in the book, and then I realized there were other stories to write as well.

2. Border Broodings

In many respects, the rather complicated trajectory I've had in my life and the kind of person I've become is a result, consciously or not, of my border experience; in many respects, I was shaped by the border. Perhaps as a New Jersey Jewish kid growing up in the shadow of the Holocaust, I developed a sense of social borders of all kinds—which helps explain the impact that the "real" border was to have on me. And of course, there is the question of Mexico—the people, culture, geography, art and spirit of Mexico. Beyond this, there is the question in this of the other side—the African and Italian Americans, the "Central American Americans," and in this book especially, the Chicanos.

As I have recounted many times, all this began much before my border days, when, as a freshman student at Dartmouth College working in the Baker Library reading room on one assignment or another, I found myself always staring up, always wondering at the incredible mural images by José Clemente Orozco on the walls. In one sense, perhaps, that's where my stories and this book began.

3

In any event, these stories are in one sense a series of meditations about experiences on the San Diego and Tijuana border throughout 1960s and on into the early 70s, as remembered and reinterpreted in the course of a life lived mainly in Chicago, Houston and San Juan, Puerto Rico. They are also stories by a Latinized New Jersey born and bred Jewish American—Latinized first on the border and in Mexico, and then "professionalized" as Latin Americans and Latinas eventually became the center of his life and career. A key assumption in these texts is that border thinking and dreaming, by creating a space for expressions of a multiple intervened and penetrated space and sense of identity, can give a certain gravity to life experiences, can help highlight human desires and frustrations lived in the times described. However, here I've just signaled an initial problem with border epistemology. To what degree does the border illuminate a life, to what degree does the very illumination process obscure important things?

Of course, the border was very different from the one occupying the same geographical space in the first several years of the twenty-first century. There were drugs but not like today. There was prostitution, but that too has changed. There was plenty of violence and there were killings. But nothing like Ciudad Juárez and now other places along the border. The border I knew was far from gentle; it invited people like me to experiences beyond our usual norms; it invited a degree of complicity in exploitation and even some degree of criminality. Despite the drugs, sex, and violence, we saw, at least some aspects of another life; some of us grew to be better people by our encounters—good and bad—with others on the border.

It is true that readers may be struck by the sexual passions on these pages, perhaps explicable by the age and situation of the protagonist and some of the characters that appear. Without a doubt we witness examples of sexism, racism, colonialism, and cultural imperialism, though I believe we can also trace the uneven but

4

nevertheless real development of the protagonist in better directions—albeit not without backsliding, contradiction and all the problems of uneven development. I might also agree with friends of mine who have read my manuscript, that my evocations of the border and travels in Mexico are somewhat thin—the travels often being a repeated lists of tourist "spots" without much sense of place except as a backdrop for steamy encounters centered on sexual or yes, male pleasure—or, in most cases, frustration.

Of course, as one very good friend, trying to defend me a bit, wrote, "The late sixties were a pre-feminist time—or rather a time when feminism was still emerging; and Mel is a character very much bound up with that time." And a question I might ask of all readers is if this book is as sexist, touristy, or for that matter racist as it may appear to some—if it's an anti-sexist/ant-racist, anti-touristy and, yes, an anti-colonialist book about a figure who in spite of all the defects and flaws we can impute to him, is one who may be able to grow and change, however gradually and unevenly, along the border road. Is this not the story of someone who perhaps thinks he knows what he sees when he only sees a small part (and that with distortion) but who gradually absorbs what he is not conscious of seeing into the he that he gradually and contradictorily becomes. Is this not somehow what is presented in the text?

Married to an Italian American woman, I had become intensely aware of the Latinos around me. My then wife was often mistaken for Chicana, and we were taken for a mixed couple—we had had some unpleasant encounters.

"Hell," I told her, "If they're going to treat us this way, we might as well identify, and learn the language."

She was all for it, so we traveled to Mexico on our honeymoon, then spent a month in Spain, then six weeks in Mexico again. Indeed, I learned some Spanish, and after my divorce, found myself frequently drawn to Mexican women in my travels and in my San Diego hometown life. I was also drawn to the United

Farmworkers Movement, attending Chicano meetings and cultural events. I even took a stab at teaching Chicano literature, and, yes, worked as a volunteer in front of supermarkets in the barrio and elsewhere, urging people to boycott lettuce and grapes.

Still, outside of my life as a young lecturer teaching English, Comparative and ethnic literature in those early years, I had no close Latino friends until the early 1970s; and I think that may explain much about themes highlighted and obscured in this narrative. From the early 1970s on, many of my closest friends were indeed Latinos, and that had to have affected how I came to see the past and how I see the present now as I write. Of course, the story also touches on my relations with Afro-American and other friends and relatives, but those relationships were in my early border years and may seem secondary to an exploration of how Latino and Latin American issues and relationships became central to my life. But as this book shows, those African American relationships were not secondary after all.

The border of those early days was to spur my imagination even before I came to live nearby and came to cross it again and again during my first marriage; it became an even more obsessive part of my life in the years before and throughout my second marriage, which took me to Central America and other Latin American spaces as well. But the border only receded in my life as my third marriage turned me from the border, from Meso-America, toward the Caribbean and its own peculiar border worlds.

I matured on the border; my Latinization and humanization processes began mainly there. I eventually left only to return from time to time; but as these stories show, I am always still there.

Whatever is said of me, whatever criticisms of these stories and their characters, whatever falsified takes or misperceptions that I may have made, the truth is that for good or ill, they represent what I saw and what I have captured in the past few years even after many changes in my life and my politics. To be sure, there is much

6

autobiographical here, but also much transformation and projection. It's also true I frequently had to decide which was more important: my intent to capture what I assume is truth in my memoir narratives, or my equally important intent to write good stories— even if I diverge from what I might specifically remember as having happened in some absurd search for a "deeper" truth. All in all, I believe both memory and aesthetics are served. I believe too that I was sometimes better and sometimes worse than the I portrayed— the he or I who somehow approximates me in these pages.

Do I fail to render the others, and especially the woman Mel encounters in his crossings and incursions? I believe I have found ways in which to hear the women's voices and other voices. But I leave my readers to reach their own conclusions—not only about gender issues but even also about genre issues I am exploring. Are these anecdotes, stories, memoirs? Do these writings cross and re-cross gender and genre boundaries? Do kthey fall between two chairs or two lines? I leave all this up to you. Let's see where you sit as you follow these border lines.

I. Black, White, and City Sweet Life

Invocation: Performance Stage after Stage

In all those years on the border in the period following his divorce from his first wife, Mel's world was African American before it became increasingly Mexican and Chicano. Continuing in his lectureship at the local state university, he explored some of the city's varied communities seeking connection on connection in the midst of growing civil rights and anti-Vietnam war struggles. Theaters, concert and lecture halls, the jazz and dance, happy hour, night and after-hour clubs, the piano and pickup bars, the boat, house and even brothel party sites—all these were the settings he could find, create or relate to, all the scenes in which he and others could perform on and off stage, in and out of the spotlight, even as he lived out his years of single life passing from his mid-twenties to some time beyond his thirty-third year, when, a student and married again, he, along with his new family, finally had to leave the space which had spread its light on him.

Mel explored more than one side of what the mexicanos called "el otro lado," but what for him was the other side of that other side which was Mexico itself. In his search, he found that it was not only the border but the city as well which throbbed like an open wound: San Diego, late to a decade's fires, but finally responding to all that was blowing in the wind ...

La Dolce Vita in el rancho chico

1.

When Mel's first marriage crashed after less than two years on the border, he realized that one of his few single male friends was Lonnie Hart, a classmate of his soon-to-be ex-wife, and a San Diego African American son of principled, disciplined parents who had taught him to be thoughtful, concerned, tolerant and committed, soft-spoken and considerate to all. Mel had a very different background and personality, and his troubled, explosive years of marriage didn't help. But he thought perhaps Lonnie could provide him with some margin of companionship and stability; so, he shyly asked to move in with him for a few weeks while he looked for his own place. To his surprise, Lonnie said yes, despite his own connection with Marlena; but the short visit turned into a few months, and when the divorce was finally worked out, Marlena gave up the house to move back to San Francisco, leaving Mel to deal with the lease. He was ready to give up the place and was cleaning it up to relinquish it, when Lonnie suggested that they share the house and continue their new partnership. Mel hesitated, since moving in meant maybe daily reliving memories of that broken marriage, but Lonnie wanted to live there—he insisted and won, though his victory was short-lived.

The house was surely unique—in a tiny valley between the southeast back end of Balboa Park, a tiny ranch-like dwelling in the Golden Hills neighborhood, a low budget, jerry-built and ramshackle structure, nothing in itself with trees and park in front and rows of houses on the bluffs above the incline in which it was set, and in front of it, a public golf course and running paths right next to the clubhouse and out onto the street which provided a majestic route back to the house—it was a rural home in the heart of the city, and it was hard to resist. So, take it they did, gradually transforming it from the home of a dysfunctional married couple to the den of two young bachelors ready to reshape their lives and the place they lived in.

Once moving in again, Mel began to scramble to find his way in the world of women. A young M.A. English lecturer teaching several international students, he knew those students were clearly off limits but that left a wide range of possibilities on-campus. Off-campus too, he could go out and seek women; he could go to Friday happy hours and try to pick someone up or, at least take telephone numbers, real or fictitious. Over the months, he could explore possibilities within the ghetto theater group he would help found, or in the Chicano settlement house, where he began to attend UFW and neighborhood improvement meetings, and over time, hold theater workshops for Chicano and Mexican kids; and he never fully left behind the jazz world of his friend Aldo; and of course Lonnie 's social work grad student friends who ended up becoming part of his world as well, now that Marlena had abandoned the field. Despite the range of his possibilities, however, he had difficulties latching on to anyone in his various areas of opportunity. Over time, his personal life came into clear contradiction with his developing politics. It was then that he finally convinced his otherwise sane roommate that they should make the most of their broad social networks by holding, say, once-a-month parties inviting one and all to their great little house.

Not only was the house itself an excellent party space, but it had ample parking up and adjacent to the long driveway that led to the front door; and there was also space in the neighborhood, along the edge of the park and in it as well—by the public golf course and clubhouse and other areas, there were places where drunken couples or pick-up dates could take refuge to consummate their little passions.

12

"What a setup!" said one of the first guests at the first party. And surely it was—not that that helped Lonnie or Mel.

That first party was small enough, but many heard about it through the grapevine and the word soon spread, so that at the second party, the house was flooded with visitors many of whom they didn't know and many of whom were unattached women also looking for dates, mates, or thrills. The parties grew ever wilder, and it was all the hosts could do to keep the pot-smoking, drinking, petty theft and screwing down to a scandalous limit. The house would fill with people, the adjacent parking areas with cars; the music would blast, the BYOB bottles would fill garbage bags and create a mass of litter mixed with cigarette buts, empty cans and condoms around and in the house. The dancing, the flirting, the hijinks, the foreplay, yes and sometime consummations would go on for hours until—and it was no easy matter—the weary hosts would urge the lingering guests to leave. And even as most people began filing out, one friend or another would call to see if things were still going on because he'd heard that lust was ablaze in a little corner of Golden Hills.

Soon enough, the parties came to be well-known bashes, with too many strangers coming in stealing books and booze, smoking dope and testing the beds for various and varied sexual encounters. But it didn't do much for the two friends. It indeed seemed the parties were designed to bring others together but leave them to their own devices. Once Mel invited a girl of interest only to see her go with another; more than once a girl he had dated without outcome came to his party, kissed him hello and then ended up with one of his friends. Even when Mel had some success at one party or another some weeks down the line, the results would be disastrous. His loneliness would lead to his accepting partners who weren't all that suitable and he'd have to spend weeks getting the women to move on, without hurting their feelings too much. Or he'd get hooked on one, who'd leave just as he was getting in over his head. At times he and Lonnie complained to each other that instead of providing them with a steady supply of romantic candidate prey, the house became where others could hook up, leaving them to clean up the house and count up missing things.

"My god," said Lonnie one night, "this is going too far, it's like we're pimping for all these people!"

All too many things happened at the parties, the chaos was too great. Lonnie's friend, Peter, showed up with a woman Mel had fallen for and lost after causing him immense pain; and she somehow felt the need to flaunt her hot new affair in his face, and end by insulting him directly before she left the scene. A young former student he invited (a prim, prudish and rather obese Italian American young woman he'd felt sorry for) entered one night and, quickly hooked up with two actors in the ghetto theater group he worked with. They charmed her with a Black Power rap and went off for a threesome that would somehow become a well-known example of the party's brilliant track record. One night they added a visiting actor to make a splendid foursome that became the talk of the town—who did what to whom and how becoming a matter of general speculation and debate. Mel would remember with remorse how innocent she'd seemed as his student, and how wild and crazed she'd let herself become with just a few drinks he'd set up for her at his party.

On still another night, a rather buxom Jewish woman arrived and made it clear to Mel that she saw him as her possible Jewish catch—a young paunchy, balding professor who she could bring home proudly to her mom. Mel considered her for a moment and got her phone number; but this night he was drawn to a young Chicana woman as cute as a button, with short skirt and pageboy hair, talking tough talk about her military service. He tried to engage her but soon realized he was barking up the wrong tree. He wandered around drinking more than his usual, and then retreated

14

to one of the bedrooms where he found the Chicana fondling the Jewish woman's breasts.

"Oops," he said, excusing himself as he made a rapid retreat. His experience with his first wife came springing back into his mind. It seemed to him that all the women he knew were becoming lesbians—that they couldn't resist. And why should they, since both men and women found women to be beautiful and desirable? What chance had a lonely and shabby he against the growing wave of she's?

He went back to the living room dance floor and found that a new group had come in the door—this time, some six guys with their semi-hooker girlfriends he knew slightly from a blues club he'd hung out at once in a moon. There was Veda, who he'd taken home one night after they did it in the club parking lot and then a second time along the Golden Hills Park circle with its beautiful view of the city and bay—he kind of went for her, but she just used his parties to hook up with one friend of his after another. There was Lula, who he'd also picked up but soon caught on (he a brilliant researcher) that she was a transsexual happy to be with a kind if gullible professor. And he even saw one of the beautiful and desirable women his ex-wife had taken on as a lover in the last wild days of their disintegrating marriage— she was brazen enough to come by and tell him in so many words, just so there would be no doubt as her charming visit developed throughout the night, that just because she'd fucked his wife, that didn't mean she'd fuck him.

Then who should come in the door but the willowy blonde former student of his who'd spent hours in his office telling him of her troubled affairs and then came by one day to confess she'd had her first and wondrous encounter with a woman who made love to her hour after endless hour—so much better, oh so much richer than her times with callow and crude males (perhaps ones such as he). She approached him now, maybe to share more lovely sentiments, but he turned away pretending not to see her.

15

He could take no more. He escaped out the door, up the stairs and the small hill leading to the backside of Balboa Park, breaking into a drunken jog, running past the public golfing clubhouse, the golf grounds and, passing the community house, where he'd seen Ike and Tina some months before the breakup. Now he turned onto the street itself that brought him back to the house and the raging party. By this time, a few groups of new people, most of whom he didn't know, had shown up. Some communal vomiting was going on in the bathroom, and people were starting to dance Motown, the Beatles, and the rest. One woman he had never seen before in his life, with a beautiful face and lithe body grabbed him and urged him to dance with her.

"Sorry, I'm not a dancer!" Mel said.

"Then how are you going to get a woman?"

"Well, I'm bald, fat, poor and soured by my first marriage, but I'll just have to plug along and do what I can!"

"The host can't dance!" announced the woman.

And then it seemed to Mel as if all the women pushed him on to the dance floor and insisted that he dance with them. He flipped and flopped from one woman to another, caught in a whirlpool, unable to stop. And then one very slim and deadly girl turned on flamenco music and led him on to the floor, where they carried out imitation gitano moves, Mel standing erect, drawing his breath in, and trying to make himself into the very image of the slim flamenco dancer he was not. Still the girl lured him into one insanely complex move after another, until he keeled over, exhausted, and outmatched, as she lifted her high-heeled shoe onto his prone body, grazing his genital area with the heel itself.

"Olé!" she screamed, and the others joined in.

Out of the corner of his blurred eye, he watched the Chicana and Jewish girl take their leave hand in hand out the front door and into the night.

16

2.

The next Monday he returned to his classes, and one of the most attractive women there, Nina, the girlfriend of a very talented, good-looking, and charismatic avant-garde Italian American director, Bob Glaudini, made her way up to him after the class.

"That was quite a party," she said.

"You were there?"

"Yes, we stopped by after our play, and watched your crazy dance."

"Oh," Mel said, not knowing what to say, thoroughly embarrassed. "I guess I was too drunk to see you," he said.

"Well, you know what I realized?" she asked.

"What?"

"That you don't have a girl, you're having trouble with women!"

"I guess you figured me out," Mel confessed.

"Well, what are you going to do about it?"

"If you weren't going with Glaudini, I'd know what I'd try to do," he answered, looking right into her beautiful eyes.

"You can forget that," she laughed. "But something's gotta give!" she warned, kissing him on the cheek and taking off for her next class.

Mel pondered his situation, the grind of class preparation and grading, the limited time for socializing, and then the panic starting on Wednesday that the weekend was coming, and he had no one to ask out and no plan he could follow. The anxiety was such that he ended up dating women in whom he had little interest, searching out happy hours, where, going alone or with a friend, he had virtually no success. The years of marriage had warped his sense of norms, what he looked for in a woman, what he hoped for in a relationship.

Turning more aggressive, Mel returned to the few jazz clubs where his co-divorcee Aldo Park and friends had various gigs throughout the city, hoping to latch on to one of the women who hung with the band. The notion of sleeping with a boss saxophone player was the dream of many a female jazz groupie, but they often had to settle for less. And that's where Mel figured he could make his mark. But the fact is he had little luck there. So, he ended up going back to using his own parties as recruiting grounds, convinced that he only way he had to win women was to draw on people from his varied San Diego worlds and to invite them to what became the second round of the notorious house parties. This time around Lonnie was less eager, as he was entering a serious relationship and fretted seeing the absurd, frantic moves of his friend obsessed with sex and adventures frittering away his writerly talents, whatever they might be, as he desperately chased one relationship after another.

The only reason Lonnie agreed was because Mel suggested they use the parties to raise money for Bobbie Kennedy, Eugene McCarthy, George McGovern, the anti-war and Civil Rights movements, black and brown. So now, the parties had a higher purpose or at least an acceptable pretext, and very different people began showing up and changed the atmosphere for the better. There was a signup and contributions table replete with pamphlets, petitions, and mailing list notebooks; people were promoting different causes and rallies. This new environment attracted professors, activists and theater people providing Mel with a new range of possible women, though, as usual, with greatly mixed results.

First came one of Lonnie's closest friends, much older than he—Ruth, a Jewish mother of two grown sons, her veins turning varicose, her hair tinged with grey—her boyfriend, an unschooled MENSA genius whom she admired and probably loved.

"Break off with him, and move in with me," he told her halfway through the party.

"Why don't you pick a fight with someone your own age," she said, rejecting his advances with a mock punch and then a kiss, laughing as she left the party early, clearly put off by its early excesses, including those of one of the hosts.

There was Judy Rosenthal, the L.A. Jewish social worker friend of Lonnie, who put him down on date after date only to go to bed with him one evening after a party where she witnessed how he flirted outrageously with his student host's mother (Judy went back to his apartment, cursed him out but ultimately made love with him, coming quite frantically, but then saying she never wanted to see him again because he was one crazy Jew hung up on Mexican women and border love—one crazy Jew she couldn't snare and control, he thought in a second of vindictive triumph).

There was Susan Mendelsohn, the young Jewish girl who, seeing a dog hit and run, moaning in pain and unable to lift its entrails from the pavement, made Mel go around the block to take the dog out of its misery (but she never took Mel out of his).

There was that other Jewish woman whose parents led a Synanon group and got Mel to participate as well, but he got no further with the woman that watching Star Trek episodes with the whole family in their recreation room. Romancing female members of his tribe was not working out.

There was Victoria, the Armenian girl, who played Dylan's electric guitar betrayal album as they made love listlessly in her big brass bed, whenever she tired of her steady boyfriend.

19

There was Caroline Bass, who played him Beatles music and bedded him only to find he didn't care for her "that way," but came to his parties to wish him well and see what or who what other catch she could snare.

Then came the African American women from a theater group he'd gotten involved in: Phyllis who looked like a spinster schoolmarm, but insisted he bed her, only to find he didn't want to take her out. Aldo Parks claimed it was because he couldn't introduce her to his mom. But, no, that wasn't it—it was just that he wasn't attracted to her; and the proof was right there when Ernestine came through the door—Ernestine, who looked like Diana Ross's younger sister and whom he'd have invited into his mother's bed, his mother present or not, if given the chance, which he wasn't, because she brushed him off like a dung fly.

He had better luck with a woman he met at a near-downtown bar, Verna, who went home with him, made love with him, and then tried to lure him into her welfare supplement program until he finally realized he was one of all-too-many contributors to her cause.

There was Sandy, the blonde long-nosed and fluffy-breasted Italian American girl, who came to the party and insisted on sharing his room for some weeks, until she left with a fury, seeing him infatuated with a Chicana who rivaled Ava Gardner and flirted with him, only to then reveal she was the girlfriend of an Anglo surfing whiz who made a fortune with his boards and took her to Bariloche ski resorts on their fabulous four-day Cono Sur weekends.

There was Linda, the UCSD campus activist who showed up and insisted on moving in, becoming his assistant at the theater and his bedmate at night, and the only way out of it was to convince her to have an affair with a younger man more her age, but confused about his sexual identity who she might be able to straighten out. For weeks he set up things for them, and she finally took him up on it and apparently resolved the confusion, leaving Mel fuming with

20

jealousy and insecurity (was the supposedly gay young man better in bed? She never answered, but never slept with Mel again).

And then came his second Sandy, the final Jewish try of his border years, a heavy eye-browed Ashkenazi woman, who exchanged phone numbers with him and then called him first, inviting him to see Zubin Mehta and the L.A. Symphony play Stravinsky and Mahler—she whose sensibility brought out Mel's lost soul—only to find that she was incapable of entering into anything with him beyond thoughtful conversation. Then one night, after a movie, she invited him in to her La Jolla apartment and offered him something stronger than pot. They sat smoking and listening to jazz, and she told him that she liked him well enough but hated men and couldn't stand four walls. He said to her he loved her, tried to kiss her, but she turned her head and retreated to her room.

He left her house and drove back south toward his part of the city blasting the Temptations on his radio, but the hashish was burning his brain, and he died for something sweet, and stopped at the all-night coffee shop on the ghetto/barrio border and ordered two pieces of apple pie à la mode and a cup of coffee. The counter was horseshoe style, and as he ate his pie and sweetened coffee, he saw two police officers sitting across from him.

"They're staring at me," he said to himself. "They can see what I'm eating, they must see that I'm totally high."

Feeling a wave of fear rising in his body, he rose, left the money due plus a big tip on the counter, and made it down his side of the horseshoe toward the entrance, where, as he turned the door handle to leave, he realized he had not taken his eyes off the policemen from the moment he stood up and started his retreat.

21

And so, he continued out the door, got into his car and headed south toward the border, when, almost too late to go back, he realized that he was too high, too broke, and out of gas, and so took the turn that led him north and east toward his apartment to spend another night alone and wait for the next party where maybe he'd meet someone new.

All the World as Stage

1.

None of Mel's border experiences would have been possible without his job, the source of the funds for his trips, and the place where he subjected his experiences to some critical distance and analysis. Of course, in all this there were the friends he made, the impact of fellow faculty and students upon him and him on them.

It was a time of great upheaval; and while his stories sometimes seem to suggest that he was oblivious to such things, still he got more involved day by day. As the 60s wore on, students organizing against the war began to turn to him for support; and he gradually responded, going to rallies and risking himself in confrontations with the police and hecklers. Then too, he was influenced by his colleagues—a Black professor who showed him the way to teaching Cleaver, Baldwin, Ellison and Malcolm X, a Chicano professor who introduced him to Chicano, Mexican and Border writing—and others who showed him the way as he, reciprocating, began showing his students as well. He ended up coordinating faculty advising services for minority students, ended by struggling to help establish African American and Chicano studies programs.

Still, through it all, there could be no doubt but that the greatest influence on him from the day he began teaching at San Diego State University, and the one person who would be with him from the first marriage into the second, the one who was most distant to his border life and who was nevertheless entwined in the critical decisions that made his world one dominated more by his border experience, was Jacqueline, or Jackie Tuvens.

2.

What was there about Jackie that enabled her to play the role she did? How did she, so distant from anything Mexican even as she shared his experience of living so near the border, come to so influence his border turn?

Well into her middle age, but now with a UCLA literature Ph.D., Jackie was a woman bubbling with enthusiasm. Very quickly, they became casual friends, sharing an interest in avant-garde and specifically political theatre à la Brecht, Dürrenmatt, Hochhuth, Weiss and others who sought a theatre of confrontation and enlightenment. This interest bound them so that if he or she went off to a conference the one could easily teach the other's classes, especially if the material were dramatic literature.

He became especially close with her as his marriage turned for the worst. And when he raised issues about his marriage, Jackie gave him her Mel opinion.

"Look, my friend, Marlena's a charming and beautiful woman, but she is ruining your life. She's not good for you, and you're certainly not good for her. It's time to get out."

Of course, that was not the only influence on him, or the only opinion offered him. Mel had to get out of his marriage; but once out, he could devote his free hours to the theater and maybe write once again and develop the career he had been allowing to fall in the dust. This was indeed the path he tried to follow, even though it never worked out the way he expected. What determined that path and deepened his bond with Jackie surfaced when she called to say that a distant relative had just died and left her an inheritance, and that she'd decided to use the bequest as startup money for a theatre company she hoped to develop for her plays, for her husband Bill's and anyone else who had something to offer. The only question in her mind was where to start her theater, and she suggested several places. But Mel's rejoinder, based on his earlier hopes and dreams, came down to this:

"Listen Jackie, if you're planning to start a nice little theater in the San Diego hills, I give you my blessing and my promise to buy season tickets and otherwise support the theater. But if you really want to make a difference in these roaring times, you need to think about getting together an inner-city theater perhaps working with poverty kids as you try to involve community members in questions of civil rights, black power, the farmworkers' struggle, and other issues facing the country and people right here in town."

Meeting with him on campus, Jackie looked at Mel shocked, because even though she was far more politically attuned than he, it had never occurred to her to try something so difficult as to develop a theater relating to a poverty community and its ongoing problems in the city and the world.

Suddenly the concept began taking off—first, a theatre exploring Black issues with Black actors, staff, and directors; then, as they could develop it, a Chicano theater dealing with farmworker, urban and immigration issues—and then a broader theater coping with problems and issues at home and abroad. As she told him her plan, she also said to him that her husband Bill went for it but pointed to all the risks—that the casts would be unreliable, that the theater would be harassed by those who didn't like its politics and social views, that few people would attend and that gradually the whole inheritance would be caught up in expenses, fines, and everything else one could imagine.

"I want you to know we're doing this thing knowing all the negative things which follow. But I want your involvement. I know our teaching load's heavy, and I know you're having a hell of a time recovering from your marriage. But now I've got to ask you to do even more—to work with us, lead or participate in workshops with us, write little plays and then as you get your edge back, try a bigger

25

one. Bill and I agree—we don't want money from you, but we do need your work and commitment."

3.

Mel began his theater commitment in much pain—the marriage had ended with a loss of esteem that was overwhelming. He had resorted to a therapist throughout the breakup and beyond, and the therapist told him he should feel proud of himself for finally having dared to leave, and he also suggested that getting back into theatre and writing might be the best thing for him.

He and Jackie had barely started looking for a theatre space when he told her what the therapist said, and then Jackie confessed that there was another reason she'd decided on her theater project.

"It's Bill—he's become impossible. He made that one Disney movie which is his main source of income every year, and he's been trying to write a novel about the McCarthy period and the blacklists—it's really got some great things—but he's terribly blocked, he's become bitter and almost a hermit, seeing nobody and no one and just moping about the house, listening to political commentary on the radio that almost drives him up the wall. I want the theatre to open him up, I want him to try a play, get involved, start to live again. And that's what it can do for you too," she added.

Mel was tempted to note that Bill wasn't out theatre-hunting with them, but he let the thought pass. Instead, they drove around the ghetto and barrio areas in Southeast San Diego, looking for a building they could use. Finally, they found a small church basement space in the heart of the ghetto, and they immediately arranged a lease and paid first and last month. The next question was developing a group—how were they going to get local people involved in the theater as actors and tech people? Who was going to train them and develop their skills even prior to their mounting any production? And who was going to offer up the first workable plays?

Gradually the answers fell into place. A student told Mel he knew a couple of black actors who were training with Sandy Levin, a retired actor-director who in turn had worked with Lee Strasberg and Julian Beck. Mel went on his own to meet the coach, an elderly but still feisty New York refugee who had decided to dedicate himself to training local black actors and manage them through at least their first gigs. One of his students had gone on to Broadway and then into Mel Brooks' *Blazing Saddles*; still another, Albert Hall, was a local star, a powerful, if stocky Sidney Poitier ready to take on any role to improve his skills, and clearly on his way to better things (he would play the boatman in *Apocalypse Now* and Malcolm X's Black Moslem prison teacher in Spike Lee's biopic). A third actor, Roland McFarland, was much less intense or dynamic on stage, but an even-handed team player able to keep his fellow actors in gear (he would go on to a career as a producer for Fox Entertainment). A fourth, Gilberto, a Panamanian Mel knew from party times, was a friend of the others, with perhaps no great acting pretensions or ambitions but quite able and willing to take on any part or job that might be required. A fifth performer was Ernestine, she the Diana Ross look-alike of his house party days.

Mel watched Sandy put the actors through their paces and got to know the coach and his students. He told them of the theater project and asked for alternative dates and times when they might be able to meet with the project director. He called Jackie and told her, "I think I just found the core for the theater company."

Sure enough, a meeting took place, and Jackie and Sandy hit it off, with him agreeing to move his workshop to the new theater site, and to work with Jackie and Mel in the development of a program involving acting, directing, tech and every aspect of theater.

Soon the core group of actors was recruiting their friends for the theater, and their friends brought in their kids and the kids' cousins and friends to found the first theater workshop. Meanwhile,

27

Mel looked for plays for kids and young adults. He sent out a letter to various Afro-American theater groups across the country seeking scripts and the addresses of writers. He wrote to several of the writers and some scripts started coming in. He also wrote a few "workshop plays"—ones that the younger actors could use to develop their skills and perhaps even perform for friends and relatives.

Jackie began combing the area for tech people and people who could teach tech. She worked up proposals for summer youth program monies, to provide salaries for the core actors as staff training the kids who'd receive minimum wage. She even met with the kids' parents to explain the program, its benefits for the kids, and also their responsibilities. She asked the cooperation of the families in seeing that their kids made it to and from the theater, and that they'd work on training assignments. She promised that they would see their kids in one production or another by the end of the summer.

The workshop courses began with Sandy coaching the core, and the core helping the kids, as Mel developed the kids' workshops, and Jackie worked up a production centered on the core, with a script she wrote about an Afro-American and African seeking housing in the deep south. Soon Mel directed and produced the first workshop show, opening with one of his schematic beginning efforts, a "micro-play" about the difficulties of human exchange, followed by a powerful little play by a black writer from Cleveland. The production was kind of lame, but the parents were happy to see their kids doing something. And Jackie's play had a good little run, with lots of professors and students coming to the ghetto theater and joining in discussion with the neighbors about the play and its message. Not that all was so sweet, because various cast members missed rehearsals as they got new jobs, and then one night Gilberto, one of the key actors in the play, was arrested for speeding and possession of marihuana, just a couple of hours before curtain time.

"There's nothing else we can do," Jackie told Mel. "You know the play, and you have to go on."

"But, Jackie, I've never acted in my life," said Mel. "Besides I know the play, but I don't know the script—it's not the same thing."

"If you know the play, you can improvise the script, and Roland will just follow your lead," she repeated in her ever positive and stubborn manner.

The worst of it was the scene where he had to play a light-skinned Uncle Tom landlord who denies housing to two Black students, treating the Afro-American "ghetto trash" worse than the African. For him to play the part, Jackie insisted on his putting on Black Face right there in their ghetto theater.

"Jackie, the audience is going to kill me, with my Jewish nose and my face blackened like Al Jolson. They're going to throw things—they might even lynch me!"

But Jackie wouldn't back off, spouting all kinds of showbiz clichés, as they blackened Mel's face, put on his bowtie, gave him his telltale cane, and got him ready to go on. And so it went, with him adlibbing a long racist phone conversation with the local Bull-Connor-like sheriff, and then turning to face the two Black students who came by in response to his "for rent" sign. But suddenly he realized that only one student, the African played by Roland, was moving toward him. And turning toward Jackie who was prompting from the wings, he heard her whisper, "Al was arrested too!"

At which point, Mel had to improvise like mad, and he had to decide right then and there whether there were two students or one, whether he'd act as if there were two or change the script. But how could he change the script when the approaching actor was supposed to carry the missing actor to the hospital, where in the next scene, the missing actor would be denied medical services. No, he decided, this actor must be the one who goes beat up to the hospital, or else the show won't make sense. So that's the way he played it. He pretended the approaching actor was the American Black, said all kinds of racist things to him, and then hit him with the cane in a rage (really hitting him because of his frustration with the position in which he had been placed) and then waving his cane toward the invisible actor at his side, shouting, "There now he got what he deserves. Now *you* take *him* to the hospital!"

At which point Roland staggered off the stage.

To Mel's surprise the crowd rose and applauded his violent improvisation. As he retreated to the wings, they demanded that he return for more applause. They wanted Roland to come out too, but Mel had hit him so hard that he couldn't come out, and Jackie had to announce to the audience that she was very sorry, but Roland had in fact been taken to the hospital as the result of an accident, that the show could not continue that night, but the audience could get exchange tickets for next week's performance, plus free tickets for the workshop show.

Afterward, she asked Mel, "Why did you strike him?"

Mel said he was sorry, but he said he was so frustrated by the situation that he took it out on the actor.

"Well, that's the story of race in the U.S.," said Jackie half-laughing. But Mel was in no laughing mood.

"You knew Al was in jail with Gilberto, right?"

"Yes," she admitted, "But I thought if I told you, you wouldn't go on at all."

"You're right there," he answered.

"So you see, I did the right thing," she said.

"But we couldn't finish the show."

"But at least we tried," she said, smiling.

Mel soon got over his anger and continued with the theater, but he was never asked to appear on stage again.

4.

As the summer wore on, Mel and Sandy worked on workshop scenes from a new script sent by Jackie and Bill's son, Karl—a big, angry, and violent play focused on Black and white relations in the Vietnam War. Mel worked with the kids in ensemble scenes, and Sandy worked on the core group who would take the essential parts. Gradually, Sandy and Mel presented the scenes to Jackie, and she then stepped in to bring the work together, with Mel serving as assistant director and prop man, and Sandy as her principal consultant and acting coach. It seemed they'd developed a pretty good working system, which reached a new level when Karl came to town, and according to Jackie, was working with his father, rewriting scenes, and adding material as he attended rehearsals and talked to the team, heard and viewed the actors, and got deep into the production. As things came down the home stretch, Mel worked the city looking for the needed props and costumes; and by August, everything was set, and the show went on—a smash that brought the theater positive reviews in the city paper and ticket sales extending into September.

Once the show was on, however, Mel gave Jackie his rewrite of a play about African American life he'd drafted some years before, and told her that while Karl's show continued, and they considered his play, he wanted to take a break and go to Mexico for a few weeks in the sun. She gave her blessing and off he went with his new Italian girlfriend, leaving ghetto problems behind and focusing on his personal life.

When he came back, Mel reported in and heard the verdict about his play. It seemed that Jackie, Bill and some new writers involved in the theatre found the play pretty well written and funny in parts, but they objected to the overall portrayal of black life that

31

seemed closer to Amos n Andy than James Baldwin or Loraine Hansberry.

"You might try to rewrite it and save it. But you can't have these characters accept their fate. They're going to have to fight their way toward something better."

Mel was sorely disappointed and, he felt, misunderstood. But they seemed pretty firm in their decision.

"No," he said, "I'll write a whole new script for next year."

In the meantime, the city had offered the theater group some funding for a one-month workshop in a gym space in a barrio community center, and Jackie asked Mel if he could take this on.

"You know some Spanish and you could learn some more," she said. "And this could be a new takeoff for you."

Mel was happy to take on an assignment that would mean his learning more about the San Diego Chicano world and its Mexican ties. He had seen the Teatro Campesino and wanted to try something in that direction but more urban. And he also wanted the chance to meet Mexican women, and this might just be the perfect opportunity for him at this time in his life. So, began his workshop and his Mexican border adventures grew and deepened throughout the year. He listened less to his jazz stations and more to the local and border Mexican stations, learning the songs of Javier Solís and other singers, visiting border and cross-border bars, dating *mexicanas* and developing a new life. During the year he worked on an adaptation of Georg Büchner's *Woyzeck* for an all-Black cast, but he also tried his hand at a play on the Conquest of Mexico, with wild effects reminiscent of Orozco and Siqueiros that he was learning from Julian Beck though more directly from Alejandro Jodorowsky in Mexico.

As the year went on, he worked with Bill on his transformation of *Woyzeck*, with Bill insisting on cuts and changes, and Mel complying as best he could. Always reluctant to show his

32

work, Bill even shared with him some scenes from his own play dealing with U.S. plots against the Cuban Revolution, so that Mel was more involved with the couple than ever, visiting their house every chance he got, participating in readings as Jackie presented scenes from plays that she was drafting, and as Mel and Bill introduced theirs.

The next summer, Jackie produced her play, *Change of Heart*, dealing with transplants and apartheid; Bill withdrew his play from consideration until the following year; and Mel tried to work up his play production, failing finally (the cast was too big, the production was past his organizational ability, and Sandy finally got Al and Roland opportunities in Hollywood).

The theater romance ended the day Jackie canceled Mel's play production; and, some hours later, he and Roland watched as Bobby Kennedy was murdered in L.A. Exhausted and disheartened, Mel retreated once again into Mexico. He never finished his Conquest play; but from that point on, he was conquered by Mexico as he got involved in UFW boycotts and other Chicano matters, with the theater retreating, along with Jackie and Bill, from his border life.

Years later, Mel would acknowledge his debt to Jackie. Above all, he remembered one day when, now married to a woman from Ensenada, he asked Jackie to drop him off in Tijuana to take the bus with his mother-in-law and son to meet his second wife in Mexico City. Jackie raced her sports car across the border and over to the bus station. Mel got out of the car, thanking her and kissing her goodbye.

"Well," she said, "now I see that you've really crossed the border, while we're still on the other side. You just do good things here," she said, wishing him good luck and then driving her hot car to the border lineup which might take her hours before she returned to San Diego.

Meanwhile Mel waited for his mother-in-law and her son who were coming in from Ensenada to join him on one of their many journeys south.

Zorba Without a Story

Roy Johnson became Mel's misguided guide in the hell of his first divorce. Mel lived dissolutely from one failed encounter to another, without any sense of direction or purpose, sometimes bringing a pickup or even a prostitute to his shared house. And as this madness continued, Mel became more and more attached to Roy.

But how can we explain the relationship? Roy was a high scorer with women, whose almost every hour and day was dedicated to their pursuit. Mel was after all a troubled and virtually paralyzed writer and intellectual who had fallen on hard times, a writer who could simply find no story to write, let alone one to live. Indeed, Roy represented all the negative qualities Mel imputed to men different from himself. Still Mel's frustrations in life were such that he found himself hooking up with Roy more and more, going with him to night clubs, checking out the local babe-scene, as Roy called it.

One thing that drew him to Roy were the sex king's bad looks. His face was triangular, and the geometry was heightened by a declining hairline that receded from a front peak backward. He had a great smile, but if you looked carefully, you'd see he was missing a few teeth and was well on his way to lifetime dental problems.

To make it worse, Roy's home was a mess. On the front lawn, he piled up assorted motor parts from a wide range of apparatuses. He had two out of commission cars plus his own beat-up van; and there in the midst of it all was a wreck of a boat he claimed to use some time for runs along the San Diego Mission Bay. His living room, kitchen and bedroom were scattered with Kentucky Fried chicken boxes, empty Colonel Sanders coleslaw and gravy cups, as well as the Colonel's French fry bags. He paid lip service to the civil rights, anti-war and ecology movements of the moment, went to an occasional rally, but his true cause was pursuing women, how to get the most beautiful, desirable women, and above all, white women, into bed—preferably theirs, so he wouldn't have to reveal or clean up his junk.

Roy would look at himself in the mirror and say, "Pretty— I'm so pretty." Then he'd put on his Tony Orlando shirt and scuffed up dancing boots, shining them some and getting ready for his night on the town.

Of course, they were quite different. Roy was the friendliest of friendly with the men as well as the women of the bar. His fellow women chasers gave him high fives and exchanged comments about the women as they staked out claims and prepared themselves for the fierce but friendly competition in which they all found themselves each night. To be sure, Roy was one of the best ladies' men in the group—a popular smooth talker and dance partner; he felt so at home talking to the women and taking them for turns on the dance floor, gliding with the music, and his partners with him, living the dream of happy gliding, the smoothest sailing, through all the race-centered discourse of their time and place. Meanwhile Mel sat apart sipping a drink or two, trying to size up the crowd and see if there some one he could latch on to, failing in most instances and in others succeeding to get through one dance but ruled out in the next round for his lack of talking and dancing skills.

"You have to learn to dance," Roy said. "You got to dance or lose your chance. There's nothing that turns off a woman more than a guy who can't guide her on the dance floor. You take the lead, you give her a whirl and with a few drinks or a joint, she's just about yours."

Roy was always handing out wise and happy words, and Mel scoffed at his clichés, but he listened. He listened but try as he might, he had trouble following the advice or succeeding with what the advice was supposed to help him to achieve. Yet, though he disapproved of many things Roy said, although he failed to really benefit from the advice, Mel persisted in listening and trying to follow his friend's inappropriate and sexist advice, as if someday he might have success. The fact was that Roy was Mel's Zorba, and he followed him as best he could.

He would frequently arrive at Roy's while he was watching his favorite shows—*Barreta,* or *Colombo,* or *Charlie's Angels, The Fugitive,* or *The Mod Squad, Chico and the Man, The Man from Uncle, Star Trek* or his favorite, *The Bionic Bitch*—as he chose to call it. Still, Mel believed that for all the junk Roy accumulated, he should really get a charter membership in *Sanford and Son.*

But there Roy would be, watching a show, almost always downing another Kentucky Colonel's pack with French fries and catsup. Roy would then tell Mel of his current situation with Squeeze #1, Jeannie, a genuine Anglo American college girl sweetheart he loved with all his heart and was untrue to several nights a week.

Half of Roy's waking hours seemed spent on finding ways to elude his true love and betray her with whoever; the other half were divided into making up for the hours he was absent and scheming to keep her bound to him while he went on with his adventures.

"Life out there's a jungle," Roy said "the survival of the fittest. And I intend to be the fittest for the rest of my life, no matter how long or short that life might be. And I want to help you, my Jewish intellectual friend, to teach you how to be a survivor and indeed a killer, because my friend, in this dog-eat-dog life it's kill or be killed. And I don't know about you, but I'd rather eat than be eaten, even if it's a matter of Kentucky Fried chicken and not Filet Mignon."

"The first thing you got to know is everyone is out for his own, and that means you the prey before you the hunter. What you must do is outfox the fox, and satisfy all your hungers, and we, my friend, are, by definition, hungry hunters always seeking the next meal. You of course think you're a poet, but you don't really believe too much in metaphors. If I talk about hunger, you thinkin' food and I'm thinkin' pussy. When I talk about pussy, I mean pussy. Food for me is pussy. And then I'll settle for Kentucky Colonel to keep down the costs, so I got more to invest in pussy. And I don't mean millions. You don't need a lotta money, but you need gas in your tank, you need to buy some lady that drink. Because you can't let yourself get cornered, you can't reduce your economy to a one crop dependency. No monoculture for this dude! Like Mr. Castro do say, you got to diversify—that's the first rule of a sound economy: diversification, multiplication and never stand still, keep your tank full so you can truck to the next bar, the next grill, the next bed, and the next girl.

"You don't want to ever let yourself get too hooked," Roy preached to him. "I love Jeannie to death, but I know too that she's a pussy like every other pussy; and I, my friend and you too if you looked deep into your own heart want to be king of the jungle. You do not wanna be pussy-whipped. So you got to keep her off balance, make her doubt you love her, make her guess you seeing other girls and getting it from somewhere else. You need her chasing you, and never the reverse. You never want to put yourself in the position of needing and begging. You always got to be in control—that's your role."

The more Mel got to know Roy, the more he marveled at his search and destroy energy. He seemed to spend every hour he wasn't with Jeannie looking for other women. He seemed always to have one or two casual bed partners and an occasional hot romance. He seemed to live in several apartments throughout the metropolitan area. "This is the apotheosis of the black man," Roy used to say, "White women can't get enough of us, and they leave white boys like you blowing air up their asses. And don't think it's cause we all so well hung. I mean, we are, but the truth is, we were slaves, and we know how a master treats a slave. That's our secret: we know power and we know control. Only we in the drivers' seat now. And you know something else? Of all the black men the women want, I'm the one they want the most, and you know why? I got no slave resentment, I know I'm king, I'm optimistic, I'm positive, I make 'em feel good, 'cause they know I treat 'em pretty good, all things considered. I mean I might not be faithful but I'm always sweet and understanding and I got my dick to back me up. I mean it's not sticking out, I mean, it's there, they can rest assured it's there when they need it and they do need it, no matter what you might think—they only human beings of the female persuasion, they got no choice in the matter. So I got my routine, I got my thang, and I line 'em up like so many ducks in a row and I go *quack quack quack, quack quack, quack quack.*

"And where does that leave *you*, my fine Professor friend? You a good guy, you cool, you one cool Jewish dude who hangs with the brothers. But when it come to women you are the sorriest sucker I have ever seen, you a lost lot, you don't know where it's at, and for all your school smarts, you're the poorest learner I know. And yet learning is your only hope. If you can't compete with the black man of the 1960s, you can become a hippie or a radical, or you can try to learn from a black man. You can become a white nigger, as my Jewish friend Norman Mailer like to say. Now, you ain't no hippie, you hardly dig marijuana and you too bald for the long-haired crew, and you sure ain't a radical really, no matter how many rallies you go to, cause you got sex on the brain, and if a bitch is good looking and giving you the eye, you're gonna forget your politics, you gonna betray the party—hell, you gonna turn in all your comrades and all your so-called principles just to get close to that bitch. And once you recognize that, my friend, you recognize that you're on Roy's turf and you got to learn Roy's rules. And you want to, my friend, cause while you a bad learner and everything I say goes against your white boy education, you know I'm right, cause you know us brothers are the kings of fuck and I am the king of my brothers.

And me, it is my historical obligation after having had all the advantages slavery has given us, and after overcoming all the handicaps it set before us, it's my proud duty to save your white Jewish ass, to always remind you that you got a body and not just a mind, that you got a dick and not just a pen, and you better well use it before it falls off. It is my duty and fate to be your friend and guide you to the promised land.

But Mel could not be led, because his feet were lead, his head was lead and he had lead poisoning. No matter how Mel tried, he could watch Roy all night, he could admire all his techniques on and off the dance floor, but he could not be or beat him. His mind/body split was too profound, he couldn't control his feet or his emotions. So even when he tried to play the stud like Roy, the women just laughed at him, or even worse, looked past or through him trying to see someone else.

"Perhaps" he thought, "it's because I'm on Roy's turf and I better try somewhere else, so he'd won't see me and I won't get lost trying to imitate him, failing, and earning his scorn. So, he'd go off to where his other friends, hung out: Artie Balon's jazz club, Lonnie Hart's social worker hangouts, or one of the Latino clubs so near his house, or even a black night club in the ghetto where he'd be one of the few whites subject to the grudging tolerance of those around him.

But no matter where he went, he carried Roy's image with him. "What would Roy say here? What would Roy do in this situation?" But the fact was, he couldn't imitate Roy and what worked for Roy wouldn't work for him. When he went to the black night club, he sensed that he was resented: "I gotta work for white

40

boys like this all week and now I even get to see him when I come to my bar to relax, and I get to see him drooling over my girls."

In the Mexican bars, he didn't dare look any one in the eye but focused on the edge of the bar counter itself, making no eye contact, and especially not with a woman sitting along the row or shooting a game of pool. He knew he should go to the Jewish Community center but couldn't get himself to go and when he would try dating a Jewish girl, she would soon reject him as too odd and offbeat, too Jewish and too much the "non-Jewish Jew." Instead, he learned to look for a Black or Latina woman and go with her to the bars where she would serve as a buffer. Sometimes that led to his partying with the girl's friends after hours or maybe even sleeping with a girl after a night's adventure. But somehow these women didn't attract him deeply and he'd risk accusations of racism just to get away.

All these efforts meant that Mel went about less with Roy, but it didn't mean that Roy wasn't still Mel's main man, displacing other friends who'd opted for a close relationship with one woman and left their searching, bed-hopping days behind.

But it is useless going on with a narrative about a friend whose life apparently involved no story. Indeed, Mel realized that Roy had no story, his life had no story, because everything in his life was set up to prevent any stories.

"Roy, let's go to a movie," he'd suggest. "Roy let's go hear some jazz."

"Are you kidding?" Roy would say. "They's not good hunting grounds. You got to go where the action is."

When Mel was going to have some weeks off, he'd say, "come to Mexico with me."

41

And Roy would say, "Look, Mel. I got a kinda business here. I got to serve my clients, I gotta be on call. I go away and break my rhythm, and my women start sniffing elsewhere. I come back and find they're gone. I got to be here keeping my business in order."

It was as if to break his rhythm and his business cycle would set him up for pain and then death—as if to keep his rhythm going, to experience no real story or narrative other than the vicious circle he had created, would enable him to have the sense at least that he could live forever.

"But then you're a slave after all," Mel said. "You're a slave to your Roy-all damn business."

"Maybe," Roy said. "Let's just say for argument's sake that you got a point. But then I also got the pussy, while you going to be spending all your savings to go driving all those desert miles without any pussy or fun, except with the hookers you pay for."

Mel could see Roy's point, but he came to realize that Roy could generate no story because his very life was dedicated to not having one. Reaching this conclusion, Mel felt no reason to continue being his friend, and no reason that he should continue thinking or even writing about Roy as his own life went on.

Which is not to say that Roy did not stay with him in some way. Even though he disapproved of almost all Roy did, still he remembered him, remembered his words of warning, his words of advice. Sometimes he would imagine what Jeannie or another, perhaps less central woman in Roy's life, might say or do to make a story happen. But he could never flesh out or actualize these faint and lifeless imaginings—perhaps because, like Roy, he could not really conceptualize the women in his life as active agents.

And it was also true that when he encountered a situation of some complexity and didn't quite know what to do, he would ask, what would Roy say, or what would Roy do? Even though he had to admit that what he chose to do was, with time, almost always the opposite of what Roy would recommend or do. Which is why his life was full of little, perhaps often trivial stories, but stories Roy could never live or tell. Because the essential story of Roy was that there was indeed no story.

This is how it seemed to Mel, and then he remembered that he had once confronted Roy with the truth he had come to know. "Roy, you've become Mr. Nowhere man living in your nowhere land, thinking all your nowhere thoughts about nobody."

Mel remembered that Roy got up and went out of his house, to his porch and then down to the yard, urging Mel to help him uncover the paint-needy and half ruined motor-boat that sat as if scrapped in his front yard.

"Let's you and me go for a ride," said Roy. "Let's go out on the bay."

So Mel helped Roy check out the boat, gas it up, hook it up to his van. Off they went to the San Diego Bay, the sun shining to its fullest, the wind blowing ever so gently, as he let his boat out onto the surf. There Roy opened the throttle of the boat, so barely skinned from prior use, and then it seemed to fly over the bay, along the waterways leading from Ocean Park and then through Mission Bay and on to Pacific Beach. Everywhere he looked, Mel saw bridges and hills, crowds and small groups of people, many of them waving from the shore as he and Roy waved back from the shabby boat that now shined as they rode on, through tunnel after tunnel, like so many tubes of light, until the boat rose majestic out of the water, streaming along as if on its way to the open sea and to the many beautiful places he would find on his blue horizon. And yes, soon they were flying over the water and Mel felt free, and so, he assumed, did Roy—never did they feel so much freedom, he mused, as when they reached out, wind and water resisting but also urging them on toward the greater world beyond.

And then Mel understood that at least at that time and in that place, Roy's not having a story was his story—a story that could enable him to survive and could just possibly lead him, in the long run and if everything worked out, to a different kind of freedom and to a life beyond his own ever so particular death. And wasn't it possible still that somewhere out there, they could both find the freedom that they felt on the waterway but had eluded them one way or another on the San Diego side of it all?

II. Love and Loss on the Border

"The Mexican border is the only major border on earth where huge cities sit across the fences from each other. ... Tijuana and San Diego ..." Extrapolated from **Luis Alberto Urrea**, *Into the Beautiful North* (New York: Little Brown and Company, 2009: 105-107).

"[In *Borderlands*,] Gloria Anzaldúa has described ... the U.S.-Mexican border... as '*una herida abierta*,' an open wound. ... At the border, the darker the shadows fall, the brighter its colors seem to shine." —**Ed Vulliamy**, reviewing Francisco Cantú's *The Line Becomes a River. The New York Review of Books* (September 27, 2018: 55).

The Last Laugh

In the long process of his divorce recovery, Mel's first instincts led him to women who somehow recalled his first wife's Italian features—her olive rich color, her deep voice, her sensuality, even if "errant." Early along his road to recovery, he hit on Lisa Serrano, a perky Italian American divorcee roughly his age who had taken a course with him some years before and now was working for a colleague just down the hall. Much lighter-skinned than his wife, who looked more Calabrese than Abruzzese, she nevertheless had that southern exuberance mixed with an eastern U.S. urban streetwise air that was all too uncommon in the border zone. He especially admired her pouting lips, her vixen-like eyes, and her ample breasts. The pair seemed to click on their first date listening to one set of music from the group his friend Aldo played with on the Shell Island turnoff to Point Loma; and then, waving at Aldo, he steered her out the door, and without hesitating took her back to his house.

"So this is it," she said, with some cynicism, "an hour of music, and now you want it all."

"Well, it's not like we just met," he explained as he turned off the motor, "I've wanted this to happen for a long time, and I was hoping you did too. But if you don't want to…"

Suddenly she leaned over and kissed him, parting his lips with her tongue; then before you knew it, they were embracing and he was running his hands up and down her body, touching her fine breasts only slightly, casually as if inadvertently passing, as he teased her into deep breathing, as he cupped her breast now insistently and then passed his free hand between her panty-hosed legs until his sensed her nub under his hand, and her breathing turn to moan and gasp, until they struggled to separate enough to get out of the car into the house, into his room and onto his bed. There he continued to stroke her rubbing his hand and fingers more and more frequently against her zone, until she helped him shed her bra and then the black pantyhose which seemed to almost strangle him until throwing them aside, he buried his head in between her legs, and gave her the oral loving his wife had never allowed him to give. It was delicious, mouthing her, make her sigh and moan and laugh— yes, she began to laugh in a kind of crazy ecstasy, even trying to escape his tongue and mouth until she could stand it no longer and came blasting and almost screaming, until she had one of the most complete and noisy orgasms she or he had ever experienced.

Later, he drove her home, and said he'd have a wonderful time and she said she did too and sighed ever so slightly before making a kind of bland but somehow fond repeat or maybe quote of the little laugh he had heard earlier. He found the laugh sexy, encouraging—a world of passion seemed to speak through that strange laugh. He promised he would call again and left in awe of their evening, and wondering where, from what low part of Palermo, Catania, or Naples—or Hell's Kitchen in New York—that crazy little laugh had come.

And so it came to pass that they began seeing each other a few times a week, going out to eat, going to movies and usually spending some small but very happy time making love together. He got to know her two children and found them as sweet and beautiful as could be. He took them to the park and to the beach, and it even seemed that a new little family was forming. They talked of their past marriages, their sense of betrayal, their hopes for better in life, and they even began to project a little bit the possibility of a life together. The summer coming, he probed her through her jeans first with fingers and then his mouth, as her kids slept in the next room, and he himself came as he felt her tremble of orgasm. And sure enough, that very evening, their passion subsiding, he felt her reaching back and blurting out a small version of her laugh, and he suddenly realized it was her little way of registering pleasure and a

48

small life triumph to herself and to the wider world—in this case, to him. He waited for the blare to subside and then, though he felt a pang of doubt, he bit the bullet and asked if she might want to go on a trip to Mexico with him, to visit a few key places and see how things might go between them. She was very pleased and kissed him but wondered if she could get her mother to care of the kids for a decent stretch of time.

Sure enough, the arrangements were made, and he booked their open-jaw flight to Mazatlán and back from Acapulco, leaving his land travel plans to be dealt with along their traveling way. What he didn't tell her is that he had arranged the trip so he could visit many of the key places he had gone with his ex-wife, his overt, conscious intention being to thereby obliterate their connection with her and opening the door to a woman like Lisa. And yet some part of him continued to doubt the relationship—and that part somehow focused on her laugh. It had some bray mixed in it, coming from some reservoir of decaying donkey; it then seemed also overlaid by a kind of anticipated or actually fulfilled lust, as if shading from bray into something deeper, at once more profound and guttural ranging down the scale from hyena to coyote or god knows what. Mel couldn't quite characterize it, but he knew the laugh was even possible in a moment of failure—a bitter version expressing some degree of pained deprivation or frustration, echoing the success shout but now as a chortling sign of regret and maybe resentment. In its smaller, more limited expression, the laugh annoyed him, pricked him; its enunciation, made him wince and wait for it to pass, but in its larger full-blown versions or variants (for it was never quite the same), whether positive or negative, it unhinged him, undermined his own sense of happiness and anticipation and made him wish he were miles away from the woman who otherwise (and perhaps in inverse proportion) seemed to attract him and be so right for him.

The first day of their trip came, as a friend dropped them at the border, where they crossed and took a cab to the Tijuana airport for their flight to Mazatlán. They spent two days on the beach sunning, flirting, and petting, retreating frequently to their room to consummate their spiraling passions. Then they flew to Guadalajara, went to a bull fight, saw the Orozco paintings, heard the mariachis in the Plaza Tapatío, inflaming their senses with tequila and a little marihuana, making love time and again in an air-condition-less and windowless room at the Hotel Morales, where he had stayed and suffered with his first wife and, as in a nightmare, which he had now once again chosen to experience with the same suffocating results.

Then in the middle of their third night, she had her fullest orgasm, laughed her enigmatic and enormous laugh, and fell asleep, waking seconds later, covered with sweat, and now saying, "Why don't we leave? Why don't we just take a bus someplace?"

The laugh and suggestion irked him, but he said, "Yes, why not?" And suddenly their intimacy disturbed him; and he realized she was right, it was best to go. They got up, packed, showered and left for the bus depot taking the first deluxe bus heading through Zamora and on to Guanajuato.

They were exhausted when they arrived and decided to nap before they explored the beautiful town, one of his favorite places in all of Mexico. But once in bed, he found her on him, aggressing him, wanting to take him as fully as he had taken her so many times before. And strangely as he lay on his back and she mounted him so completely, he heard a laugh issuing from his own mouth that somehow, inexplicably combined his own normal (and probably not so attractive) laugh with one that uncannily and quite involuntarily sounded like hers. Suddenly he lost his erection and stranded his lady on a staff that no longer was. But desperate for her pleasure she drew away only to mount his leg, rubbing herself against it, roughing him up to meet her not easily satisfied needs, until, not finding all she wanted in this, she finally lifted her body and planted her clitoris right on his mouth, until, perhaps more fully than with penetration, she approached the climax she had sought and desperately needed, and, now, reaching it, began to laugh that laugh which somehow turned into a hymn of great triumph and lust in which, as much as he abhorred its occurrence, he now found himself joining all too fully.

Now lying in bed with her, he found that her body that he had thought so pleasingly voluptuous—*or zaftig* in the picturesque language of his people—was rather fat; her short and shapely legs began to look fat; the penciled in moon-shaped curve of her eyebrow, the over-gunked curve of her lashes, her over-reddish brown hair and above all her over-light skin, too far from the olive complexion of his beautiful if awful first wife—almost everything about her seemed wrong. No physical beauty himself, bald and overweight, with legs that narrowed from his enormous calves to his skinny lower joints, he mourned his having fallen in with a woman who was too far from his image of beauty, who topped all her defects off with a horrendous laugh and who now was infecting him with the same unbearable sound that might follow him all the rest of his days and nights.

Of course he said nothing but as they dressed and walked out on to the beautiful central square they had seen from their window, he found his eyes wandering toward the beautiful young women who circled the plaza while the young men (mere boys, he thought) circled in the opposite direction, Mel wishing he were one of those young men instead of the shabby and forlorn Jewish intellectual without religion or deep roots that he was—and that one or maybe more of these beautiful women, and not this pathetic, inferior version of his Italian dreams, could be his. By the time he reached Acapulco, he realized he'd be happy bedding with any number of Mexican prostitutes rather than with Lisa, who seemed to almost love him and care for him and for whom he felt only a growing sense of antipathy. He could not explain it, he seemed powerless against the magnetic pull of these Mexican women who so excited him and who (he was told) were so difficult to win over.

He tried not to let on his true feelings, acting toward Lisa as if nothing had changed. And yet she must have felt something. There was that terrible moment when she turned to him in a clear gesture pointing toward the bed, and he rebuffed her, saying they had so little time and they should explore the city and its beaches. How different it all was from his first date, where he'd practically ripped off her panty hose and tongued and mouthed her until he thought he'd die and she with him; how different from all the times when he explored oral and once even anal passages with Lisa, doing all he had never been able to do with his sex-crazed but highly specialized and selective first wife, until Lisa became almost a sex slave, swooning as she pressed his hand or tongue toward where she most craved his touch. But here he was, now not wanting her, friendly but not inspired and indeed totally turned off when out of her growing nervousness (the best symptom that she was aware of something) she or he made some comment that sent her rocking with the laugh which now sounded hideous and which, now when that laugh had come to shape his own, made him wish she did not exist in his world—so that he would be free to speak a new language and pursue the women who now haunted all his waking and sleeping hours. There was nothing he could do about it; he just went through his paces, was amicable until their arrival back in San Diego, and then, felt a tremendous sense of relief as he dropped her off at her house, kissed her tenderly (he sensed it would be their last) and made his way home.

He didn't call her for several days, and then when she did call and asked about his silence, he was at a loss to say anything. "What's with you?" she asked. "We had such a great time, and now you're so distant."

"I don't know," he said, "I guess I was overwhelmed with all the work that had piled up and then, I guess I felt empty and not wanting to talk to anyone." When she persisted, he claimed that he was feeling the' effects of his divorce, that he was strangely missing his wife, that getting close to her had made him all the more entangled with the memory of Marlena, that he simply couldn't seem to give her up in memory.

"Maybe it's because I'm Italian," she offered out of her bewilderment.

"No," he said, perhaps lying.

"Well, maybe it's my laughter," she said, shocking him, because he had never mentioned a thing.

"What do you mean?"

"I don't know, but my first husband complained about it, said he hated it especially after I came, as if he couldn't stand my womanly pleasure."

"Maybe that's it," he said to himself even as he firmly denied this as a reason. For what could be farther from the truth? At least consciously, he glowed with her sexual pleasure even if he didn't like the sound of laughter which all too often accompanied it. And could it be that his first wife had indeed spoiled him for the joy of a heterosexual woman's healthy and life-affirming orgasm? Could it be that he simply could not endure her blatant expression of sexuality?

"Funny," said Lisa, suddenly sullen with the loss of her illusion of growing love, "You have your own little laugh," she said, "in case you didn't know. I didn't notice it at first, but then I did, and it began to sound more and more like mine—as if you were making fun of me or becoming too much like me. I wanted to ask you about it, but I guess I felt I couldn't broach the subject." And indeed, he recalled how he had come to the point when in hearing her own laugh in his, he seemed to lose all his desire and sought

53

some way to shake her influence. But he, even more than she, had remained silent; and, somehow, they'd lost even their thread of communication. And now there seemed to be no way to repair the thread, which was becoming a shred, especially since he no longer had any wish to repair it.

And now too, as he all but confirmed this state of paralysis by the longest of telephone pauses, she said "Well, if this silence is where we are, and if you don't think you can talk or want to see me, I guess I can wait a while to see if it's a passing thing, but don't make me wait too long. I'm not that young, I know what I want, and I'm not going to sit pining for you forever."

"Yes," he said, he understood, yes, he wouldn't wait too long, yes, he'd be calling her soon—and yes, he'd had a wonderful, memorable time with her, and he didn't want to lose her from his life. He said all this consciously lying about everything and without any intention of calling back this woman who, perhaps of all the women in his life up to that point, had shown more fascination with him and love for him than any other.

Perhaps Mel was not really lying when he fabricated his story about his lingering love for his ex. Perhaps rejecting this Italian American woman was somehow an act of revenge against all that his Italian American ex had done to him. But there was no way that this or perhaps any Italian American woman could affect him in this phase of his life. He could neither understand nor control the turn of his passions. Was it that *mexicanas* seemed less worldly than were Italian women? *Or was there some special connection with his errant sensibility that sent him in this direction? Was this a Jewish fascination with Catholics extending from the old world to the new and now veering south? Was this just a further phase of his foolish attempt to escape his history, or to fold his own group story of persecution into a wider one of others? Was it a search for the exotic?* He couldn't put his finger on it, as much as he might accuse himself of racism, cultural imperialism, and the like. But so it was, and so it would be for some time to come, with himself powerless to prevent his move from Italian to Mexican and more generally Latin American objects (or were they somehow—would they become—*subjects*?) of passion and love.

A few months after his conversation with Lisa, as he continued an all but pre-doomed campaign to latch on to a Mexican woman like those he saw in the plaza of Guanajuato, (or whatever he could garner in his border world), he ran into a former student of his who told him to his surprise and dismay, "You know I'm dating your ex-girlfriend—Lisa Serrano, We're really hitting it off, and she told me about you and how you dropped her like a potato pancake. She says she felt really bad, but that she's ok now and happy with me. I think we're heading toward marriage, and I just thought you should know."

"Thanks," he said, and wished them both well.

Actually he took the news to heart, and before the young man could go his own way, Mel just couldn't resist. "By the way does she still have a kinda crazy laugh that, well, it's really unique..."

"Oh yes," said the friend. 'It's a great life-affirming laugh. In fact, that's what led me to push her about her relationship with you, because, I swear, the only other laugh I know that's anything like it is yours."

"Really," Mel questioned. "I thought I was getting it from her."

"Well, maybe she had it on her own, but it's kind of like the laugh I always associate with you from your earliest teaching days when sometimes you even seemed happy. I guess you made a big impression on her, because that laugh's become more and more a part of her and gotten bigger, I think, since you and she dated. It's one of the things about her I most love."

María de la Frontera

1.

Víctor Tapia was the poverty program director who coordinated projects including the Mexican American theater workshop which Mel was trying to develop. An Arab Mexican lady's man who always dressed to the teeth for his job, always with fancy jacket and silk tie, shined shoes and a hot red convertible in his reserved parking lot space, Tapia was always leaving the office to meet one woman friend or another.

After a few weeks, around two on a Friday afternoon, Tapia said to him, "You like the Mexican ladies, right? I mean, you're not just here for the *amor de teatro*, right? I mean you wouldn't mind meeting a beautiful señorita, right? And you wouldn't mind helping me out, doing me a favor, right? …. Because you do me a favor and I do you one, right? One hand washes the other, right?" he said winking at Mel, and putting his cologne-scented hand on Mel's shoulder.

"Look," Tapia went on, "I got a real problem on my hands— this one and this one," he said, lifting his hands in the air, and then lowering them, with one coming to rest again on Mel's shoulder…The thing is, my number 1 girl, you know? She's got wind of this other girl I've been playing around with and she says I got to end it. And to tell you the truth, this other girl, she's ok, but she's being a real pain in the ass about all this—I guess I'm so hot, you know, she just won't let go. Look," he said, luring Mel to the back basement window of the church and pointing him toward his convertible and the woman seated therein right across from where Mel himself was parked. "There she is in my car. She's just sitting there pouting. She won't get out and won't let me go. What do you say, you come over with me and I introduce you, and you can

56

practice your Spanish on her, and try your charm on her, so maybe you can get her out of my car, and I can go on my way."

"And what do I do with her then?" Mel asked looking at what seemed to be a very pretty, red-haired Mexican woman sitting in the convertible, Mel intrigued and tempted without even seeing her clearly. "Then you can do what you can. You can try and take her to your place and if you don't really want her, or even if you do, you can take her to her place. Do it for me, Mel, I'll really appreciate it, you'll have a friend in me for life and maybe even a new girlfriend, your own Rita Hayworth, who knows?"

All this time, Tapia lured him slowly up the back staircase, out the door and into the parking lot, moving toward the convertible, where the woman was sitting, a Mexican radio station on in the car, her fingers tapping out the rhythm on the dashboard. The woman had a beautiful, angular face, and Mel even liked the freckles that crossed the ridge of her nose. But she had a very angry, disgusted look, way beyond a pout. Apparently, she understood she was being dumped and was not taking it lightly.

Mel held back as Tapia went up to the convertible and said, "María," and then rattled a string of words in Spanish that Mel couldn't understand. Meantime, María kept tapping her fingers and staring not at Tapia or Mel but at the wall in front of which the car was parked.

"Mira, María," Tapia continued, "Eso es mi amigo, Mel. Es muy buen tipo (This is my friend, Mel—he's a good guy)," Tapia began and continued in Spanish. "He'll take you where you want, María, because I have to get going." María kept glaring and Tapia finally, threw open the door. "Mira, this can't go on like this. I gotta go," he went on in Spanish, "and you can't go with me."

And with that, he literally yanked her out of the car. "Dejame!" María screamed, "Leave me alone," she repeated, now in her heavily accented but clear English). And Mel suddenly saw her more fully, saw her medium height, her orange summer dress but the very skinny legs and arms of a woman who may have been small-boned, but seemed to have been underfed her whole life. She could not have weighed more than a hundred pounds. "Mira, this guy is good people," Víctor continued in Spanish. "He's a gringo, it's better for you. He's almost in love with you already." He then reached for his wallet and handed her what seemed to be a lot of money. She threw the bills on the ground, and spat at Tapia, as he hopped into the convertible and turned on the motor "Don't worry," he said, as he wiped the saliva off his face and started backing out, with her still holding on to the car door, as if trying to get in and then sent flying from the door as Tapia pushed her away even as he switched from reverse to forward, and sped out of the lot.

"Son of a whore!" María cried, "Fuck your mother!" she shouted, trying to stand, but only remaining crouched over, crying but also gathering the money she'd refused, showing her skinny legs and knees as she picked up the bills and stashed them in her bra.

Mel tried to help her gather the last dollars, and watched as she stashed them. Now he and María faced each other in the lot, her crying, and him feeling quite moved by her cries, her curses and torments, as well as her emaciated but somehow attractive looks. Mel tried to put his hand on her shoulder, as if to console her, but she threw off his hand. He tried to communicate with his raw Spanish, and she answered him with her even rawer English.

"He had to go," Mel tried to explain, "and I said I'd see you'd be okay. Me llamo Mel," he added.

"So what?" she answered, "you think I care? He give me to you so you can just fuck me an' leave me in the street,"

"No," he said, somewhat shocked at her directness and crudity, so distant from the way he imagined a pretty Mexican town girl would talk to him, but rather accurate in her grasp of the situation. "Eres bella, and I'd love to make love to you," he

58

admitted, "but I'm not here to fuck you. I thought maybe we could go for some drinks and then get you something to eat."

"I not hungry," she said, "and don't think you can get me drunk to fuck me." But there she was, actually following him as he moved toward the passenger seat of his car. She stood there a second uncertain what to do, looking around at the parking lot and the streets beyond. What choice did she have? Mel realized, and with a dismissive gesture of her arm and a pout on her face she got into the car, plopping down, surrendering what remained of her defiance, and, with folded arms and feigned, pouting indifference, awaited as he entered the driver's seat, closed the door, started the car and began driving out of the lot.

2.

They rode on for a while, leaving the barrio behind, as Mel tried to figure out where to take her. For a while she just stared out the window and resisted any effort to talk. Then she turned on the radio and punched one car radio button after another.

"Puro gringo!" she said snidely, after listening to station after station. But Mel retorted by hitting one and then another of his programmed selections, finding his favorite Mexican stations at the end of the row of choices. She listened to one then another and then turned off the radio. There seemed no way to make small talk, so Mel just drove her over to one of his favorite piano bars that began its happy hour early. They went in and sat away from the bar but downed one margarita and another. Soon María stopped pouting and put her hand on Mel's head. "Calvo, calvito, bald!" she exclaimed, laughing almost affectionately. "Gordito, fatty" she said taking a squeeze of his all too ample belly. She then took off his glasses and put them on, making funny faces, squinting, looking over and under the rims, then putting the glasses back on his nose sliding the frame down to the tip, peering at him and stretching his mouth with her two forefingers so he imagined he looked a bit like Mr. Magoo. To top it all off, she squeezed his nose. "So big —

59

narizón," she said, and then put her hand on his thigh quite near his penis and asked. "Y so big?" They both laughed, but she then broke into tears. "Este hijo de puta, this son of a bitch, he left me. He give me to you like a bag of rice," she said. "Y ahora que hago yo? What I do with my life?"

Mel felt her pain but could only order another drink and give her a handkerchief.

"Sí," he said awkwardly, not having any idea of who she was or what future, if any, would be theirs. "Amigos, no?"

"Amigos," she said, and then she reached over and kissed him on the cheek, and then on his mouth, probing with her tongue, meeting his, returning her hand to where she had placed it before.

"The first thing a fat friend does for a skinny one is take her out to eat," said Mel, driving over to his favorite Italian restaurant, where he had her eat a plate of pasta plus half of his and all the wine she could drink, so that she became more relaxed and seemed to forget her problems for a while, eating away, he enjoying her enjoyment and enlivened spirts.

The dinner over, and on the road again, he asked her if she wanted to go home, and she simply said she had nowhere to go and wasn't he going to take her home to fuck her? "Well," ok" he said, "but I wouldn't put it that way."

"How you wanna put it?" she said laughing with a certain sadness. "And I stay with you tonight?" she asked.

And all he could say was "yes."

He did not live alone, but it didn't matter. His roommate Lonnie and his girlfriend were out, and he showed her around their little home—an urban place as rustic as one could imagine.

"He's no millionario," she said sharply, perhaps disappointed (but didn't his appearance and car say it all?). "I not marry you," she half-joked, turning to face him.

60

He found her somehow charming and attractive, he reached over to give her a kiss. She returned, kissing him playfully and caressing him, but then turning around. "I need a bath," she said, "before anything." With that he got her a towel and some soap and turned on the tub water. When it was part full, she quite naturally took off her outer garments; and, bra and panties still on, she turned to enter the tub. Suddenly she looked skinnier than ever, so much a matter of bones with a fine angular face on top of the slimmest neck. In she went, hardly causing the water to rise.

"Aren't you going to take off your underwear?" he asked.

"Solamente si tu bañas con migo," she said—only if he bathed with her and, he presumed, helped her take off her clothes. So, first, off came his things, all of them except his shorts, and she moved forward in the tub so he entered behind her. "And you still in your *chonis*—your shorties," she laughed.

"You can take off mine, after I take off yours," he said, already excited, embracing her, holding her small bra-held breasts, as she leaned back against his erection and he kissed her, gradually removing her bra and then her shorts, fondling a nipple with one of his fingers and moving his other hand toward her genitals, until she stopped him and turned him around in the water, kissing him and laughing, poking at his erection and finally taking off his shorts and clearing away the soap until she kissed and sucked his penis, spitting out remnants of soap and even singing snatches of ranchera songs between sucks and kisses while he gently massaged her back with a soap-filled cloth, until they both felt the excitement flood their senses and they rinsed off quickly, wiping and drying each other, feigning to touch genitals and nipples by accident as they ran out of the bathroom, and onto his bed, where they proceeded, ruffled sheets and all, to suck and tongue and squeeze and pant and soar and roar as they kissed and clutched and then sixty-nined like avid divers into the deepest waters and until they were both

61

overwhelmed by what seemed to him to be the grandest orgasm of his orgasm-famished life.

3.

They slept late into the morning almost wrapped around each other, Mel awakening to find her already awake and making a small racket in the kitchen, where she was working away scrambling eggs, sausage, and not chorizo. the beans already boiling on the stove.

"María, you didn't have to," he said, going up to her, giving her an affectionate caress. "You don't have to do this," he said.

"But this I do good," she said.

"Entre otras cosas—among other things," he said, still excited. But then he paused and sat down, watching her skinny arms and her legs too working away, cleaning up a kitchen mess even as she cooked up a storm, enjoying doing these domestic chores, proud in her work, perhaps, he couldn't but reflect, because she had never gone to school, and making love and doing domestic chores were all she knew. And then it occurred to his theatrical mind, "but maybe she thinks this is a tryout."

Suddenly he grew nervous about this dubious gift from a dubious "amigo." What was he to her but a possible solution, a line held out to her after she'd been tossed back into the sea. This was one fish who perhaps longed to be caught. "How long you've been living in San Diego?" he asked.

"I no live here," she told him. "I work here some time. Víctor got me a job cleaning house for this gringo couple. I work for them and then I go home to see my baby." So she was a border girl, Mel realized, with one foot still over there and maybe trying to get a foothold here. Víctor was no longer a possibility, but maybe he was. And in fact, he was excited to have her with him, the first Latina woman in his life after all his fantasies during his Mexican travels. But what could he do with her reality? Who was she? Could she be expected to have any real feelings for the funny looking man who

62

she mocked, though with some affection, even in the midst of her sense of abandonment and humiliation which was so overwhelming the day before?

Mel could not help but be fascinated with the way she dealt with the hand dealt her, her apparent happiness bopping around the kitchen only hours after Tapia's terrible ploy. He could not help but think of the many miseries she must have known in her life that left her so skinny and abused so that she could efface and recover from her humiliation just the day before, so that making this strange, funny gringo breakfast and cleaning his kitchen mess filled her with pleasure and, perhaps, hope.

Now moved but wary, Mel took his seat as she served him the breakfast, giving him a kiss as she poured him some coffee, and finally sitting down at his side. He asked her about where she was from, about her family and her current life. She came from a small town in the state of Durango, she told him, a place on a curvy road from Mazatlán, remarkable because all the buildings were of wood and not adobe, a place too, she added, of poverty and ready alcohol, famous for macho men and passive females exploited to the maximum. She told of her mother's troubles, the sufferings and cruelties of her siblings, the advances of predatory relatives and neighbors, and her decision finally to take bus after bus, moving up Mexico's west coast and then through the Sonora dessert, finally turning west to Mexicali and Tijuana. She had lived there some three years, she said, had her little girl there and did what she could to support them, until she met Tapia, who claimed he loved her, getting her a counterfeit card that she could use to commute back and forth across the border, and, even getting her a job with the elderly San Diego couple so she wouldn't be obligated to him, and could build a life for herself with or without him.

"But it didn't work out that way," Mel suggested. Despite all, she had grown emotionally dependent on Tapia, and while she worked for the couple, she waited for him to come by to take her to a motel or wherever, making love with him and maybe seeing if she could get him to commit himself further to a life with her. But that never happened, and lately she'd felt more and more used and abused by him, even to the point where he would bring along his latest girlfriend and tried to set up a three-some and other special arrangements, until, these efforts were vetoed not by her (she apparently didn't feel she'd much choice about them) but by the new favorite girlfriend, who also pressured him to do what he would probably have done at some time anyway: drop her completely.

So here she was, and here they were, Mel embarked on his first real Latina adventure and encountering a situation which seemed anything but exhilarating, entering him into a world of poverty and misery, of violence and even bondage. He looked at his new lady love and her body marked by deprivation and brutality. Increasingly he felt more compassion than passion, thinking of her life and his possible part in it. It all looked so difficult if not impossible. The very forces that had shaped and limited her life would prevent their full coupling. What could he offer her except his sympathy, and as his sympathy grew, the more his sexual impetus would wane; and once that happened, what would they talk about, what could they share except a sadness about the harshness and cruelty of Mexican life? What possible future did they have, especially given his own relatively marginal situation in the economics of his own country?

Almost involuntarily, he found himself continuing his inner dialogue out loud: "And now, us. María and me—¿que hacemos,? what do we do?"

"Up to you," said María, gathering up the plates. "We make love again, no? and then you take me home, and I come back Tuesday to work, and you tell me what we do, ok?" What a relief for Mel to have any decision delayed, what happiness he felt as he returned to the bedroom with her, turning his empathy and concern into a tender sea of feeling that led them both to the edge, especially as he caressed and sucked her tiny breasts, while reaching into her panties until they both felt their passion rising on the tide.

Afterwards, as if following her orders, he drove her toward the border, stopping to buy some things for her and her daughter, and then continuing to San Ysidro, where she told him he had no need to cross and face the huge line of return traffic he'd encounter. She wrote down his number and said she'd call him the next week.

"María," he asked, "what's your daughter's name?" She said the name, but he didn't quite grasp it.

Then she kissed him again and said, 'Gracias for being a sweet muchacho. I can leave my job and clean your place and we can make love all you want—you think about it," she said, exiting from the car and making her way, packages in hand, across the border.

4.

In the days which followed, Mel tried not to think about her, but he couldn't quite get her skinny body and birdlike legs out of his mind. His previous girlfriend, Lisa, called to ask if he had worked out his thoughts and he told her no, but he thought it was over.

"Is there someone else?" she probed.

"No," he said, but he didn't know if he was lying or not. Of course this affair could never be. "It would have to stop before it begins," he thought, citing one of his favorite Sinatra songs, no matter how much under his skin she might get. And yet he wondered what would happen if she called or she appeared; and if he couldn't resist making love to her once and then again, how would he extricate himself from the relationship, and what would happen to María and how he might be or feel about it all?

65

One morning he dreamed of her, dreamed of holding and making love to her. He awoke, rubbing himself against his pillow, nearing orgasm, when María, having found the front door open, strode into his room only to see his naked buttocks thrusting against the pillow.

"*Cochino*! Dirty pig!" She cried out, laughing as he turned and instinctively covered up. "You masturbandose pensando en mí!"

"María !" he exclaimed.

"Jerking off thinking of María , when you could have me any time you want," she said, uncannily.

"Come here," he urged her, standing now, his erection beginning to return. And as if in a dream more intense than the first, she did come over to the bed and let him have her, fondling and sucking hard on her nipples, exploring her here and there, until she arched her body and rubbed herself against his open mouth forcing him to make her come, just as he reached an orgasm of his own.

"Agh!" she cried out, but got up quickly. "I just come to see you, *cochino*, to say hello. The old man and his wife, they waiting outside—see if you can live without me, because no one fucks you like María."

5.

Several days passed and he began to wonder if he'd ever have a chance to see her again. What happened, why didn't she call? He kicked himself for not having gotten the number of the couple she worked for. He thought of calling Tapia, but he didn't really want him to know how involved he'd become with his reject. Just the thought of his motivations disturbed him to the point of nausea, and he was getting lost in it, when María in fact called him.

"Can you come get me?" she asked. And he said yes, driving to a small San Diego suburb, parking, and knocking on the door of the house she mentioned. Out she came running, a suitcase and a bunch of packages in hand. "*¡Muevate!* Get going!" she almost shouted as she got her things and herself in the car. "Get me outta here!" she urged him, as he sped away.

"What happened?" he asked.

"They treat me so nice, but then they show themselves. They want me to sleep with them, make love to them both, *la mujer* more than the husband. Ay! *Que asquerosos*, how disgusting," she said, spitting out the window.

"I never going back there," she said, starting to sob. And then, before he could respond, she said, "Mira, what do you say? Do I come with you now?"

"María, I can't afford all you need for your daughter and life in Tijuana, and I don't want us to set up house only to find out we shouldn't be together." She looked up at him but didn't seem to see his point. To her, Mel supposed, you take what chance you have and make the best of it, and if it doesn't work out, you go on to something else if you can. For him, on the other hand, you were wary of entanglements that could affect your life for years and maybe ruin your chances forever. As much as he was attracted to her, and as much as he did in no way wish to hurt her further in life, he couldn't satisfy her wish for an immediate solution and possibly create a hell on earth it would be so difficult to escape. Didn't all his experience teach him this? Wasn't it the truth of his terrible first marriage and the consequences he was still paying? Wasn't this truth a virtual law of the jungle?

"I won't charge you much, I make your house nice, I make love to you like your own little gatita—your little pussy," she said.

"Look," he said, "the money's one thing, but hay las complicaciones—it's not that easy, we have to know each other better and see if we'd have even a chance to make it."

"Then take me to the border," she said. That's where I belong any way. I got your number, you see if you don't miss me, if you can live without María —see what happens to you," she said, defiantly but also with bitterness. "Cause I no want nada de nadie. If you don't want me, I don't want you, I don't want nothing from no one."

She turned toward the window, and when he reached out to touch her arm, to console her or just to see her pretty face once again, she waived him away, and just watched the signposts as they moved once again to the border where, once again, too, she got out with her packages and said, "I call you some day and see how you like your life without María ."

6.

The weeks went by, María lost to him in whatever life she had on the border—in Tijuana itself or wherever. Mel, still without a number to reach her, sought other dates, other relationships with Latinas or other women. But through all his efforts to forget and to live, María lingered on his mind—her difficult life, her choices, and efforts. What had happened to her? Would he ever see her again? And sure enough, one day, when he had almost lost hope in it happening, she indeed called him.

"¿Como estás?" she asked.

"How are you doing?" he asked her.

"Aquí estoy—a waitress, you say?"

"Where?" he asked.

"Aquí," she answered. "Here in el Bar Diana in Tecate."

"Can I come and see you?"

"You just come to the club any night except Monday," she said, "and ask for María."

He went that very night, crossing the border at Tecate, and driving just two blocks to a bar located on the west side of the central plaza and just a few blocks from the famous brewery. He knew the bar from a fiesta he'd gone to with his first wife. He was relieved to remember it was not your regular hooker bar, even though one might buy a willing girl out of the bar to spend some time with her. Entering, Mel realized it had gone downhill over the years. There indeed seemed to be some hookers. But the waitresses didn't seem to be among them, he surmised happily, as he spied the skinny girl of his dreams serving some young men at almost the opposite end of the counter.

Soon enough she came over to him. "Look who's so fast to come see me. You still like me a little?"

"Never stopped," he said so happy to see her pretty face, so sad to see her still so skinny frame. "Can you sit with me?"

"In a little while," she said. And sure enough, she served out drinks to all her customers and finally came to sit by him, asking the bartender to serve her a tequila and openly taking his hand and kissing it, as her way of saying hello. They sat drinking and not talking much, because the music was so loud.

"You have a new girlfriend?" she asked.

"No," he answered. "And you?"

"Mel, I got no girlfriends," she said laughing, with him joining her but noting that her English had somehow improved and wondering about her probable teachers.

"Why Tecate and not Tijuana?" he asked.

"Cause Tijuana too nasty," she offered. "Too many putos y pimpos."

"Too many male prostitutes and pimps," he echoed, thinking over her meanings with care. "Better mezcal than mota. Better Coca Cola than cocaine," he said, and she laughed, though not without some troubled silence he sensed creeping into their patter.

The music changed to something softer, and he found himself stroking her arm, and then touching her face. "I've missed you," he said. "I've never gotten over you."

"Me too," she said, kissing his hand again. "My funny muchacho dulce—sweet boy," she smiled purring. The music turned up and she said, "Give me $30 for the manager and I go with you—for the night." she said. He quickly laid out the money, she handed it over, and they walked out the door oblivious to everyone. Reaching his car, she kissed him hungrily and he returned in kind. "Take me away from here. Vamos a Ensenada. It will be like our *luna de miel*—our honeymoon."

And so it was. They drove southwest down the old curvy road through the Guadalupe Valley from Tecate to Ensenada, holding hands as they turned this way and that on the long ride past a few Indian villages and towns and even an Indian *ejido*, arriving finally almost at midnight, to see the coastal lights of Ensenada.

They drove around town, stopped on the Juárez for some tacos, moved into Housong's Bar for some quick drinks, and then settled into a French motel across from the town's fine French restaurant. In the room, they drank some more, kissed and cuddled watching a movie, and then moved into the bathroom to shower.

"No bathtub here," he said to remind her. "I'll never forget our wonderful night."

"This will be sweeter," she said, as they entered the shower and he began to scrub her back, rubbing his erection against the crack in her moon. Soon she turned and kissed him, gripping his

70

penis firmly. Then she kissed him, and he felt something acrid on her breath; he smiled; and she returned his smile, while he could not help but note several bruise marks on her arms and thighs, the skinniness of her body—the abuse of her, perhaps by others who paid the $30 to get her out of the Diana.

Abruptly, she left him to shower and took her towel with her into the bedroom. He took some time washing, enjoying the warm water but brooding over the damaged woman, who was supposed to provide the crazed, thrilling pleasure they were slated to share soon enough. But when he came out of the shower, dried himself and entered the room of their joyous consummation to be, he found her sleeping and snoring softly on top of the bedcovers. Somehow, he felt relieved, as if a burden had fallen off, as if he had perhaps dodged a fatal encounter. As deftly as possible, he slid the blanket out from under her and then over her so she could rest better. He turned to the bathroom and looked for a cigarette in her purse, finding an open pack among other odds and ends here and there. He lit a cigarette and sat on the toilet seat, looking at the various items and resting his head on his hands; troubled and saddened by these signs of her broken, difficult life. He saw a few small card-size slips of paper with what must have been her phone number on each and took one just in case. But what could he really offer her? Could he really imagine living with her? What would they talk about after a time? What could he do to help her if he knew now that the intense passion he felt for her would wane and the relationship would have to die?

He pocketed the phone number slip, but put everything else back in her purse, put on his pants and went out to his car, looking up at the moon over the Pacific and cursing his life, cursing Mexico and all that happened to people under this same moon. Then, exhausted and resigned, he returned to the room and his snoring princess, lying down beside her, giving her the most gentle and pained kiss, and then falling into a deep sleep.

8.

In the morning, they awoke and embraced. He didn't mention their failed evening, nor did she; instead, she stared at him, her expression almost blank. "So what do we do now?" she asked him.

"You want a beautiful breakfast?" he asked.

"Sure," she said, "Why not?" They gathered their things, and he took her across the street to the French restaurant and she tried an omelette with paté and then some of the wonderful pastry. "We could have this life," she said, "if only you want. We could *vivir juntos—sí*, live together if you'd let me," she answered.

"Maybe someday," he said.

"Someday," she repeated in bitter contempt. "*Hipócrita*," she said grinding her remaining pastry into the plate. "We gotto go," she said after a time. She had her daughter waiting for her in Tijuana. And then he said nothing, paying the bill and walking her to the car.

He began the trip to Tijuana, driving along the spectacular toll road, driving erratically, faster, then slower, around curves making jerking moves even along the most beautiful and dangerous parts of the coast. He looked toward her, and she was trembling softly.

"María I've missed you every day, I want to keep seeing you," he said.

"Every day you fucking with someone else and you say you want me, but you don't want me."

"I've missed you and every day I think of our lovemaking and every day I want us to be together, and then something holds me back."

"And now you hold back, because I fall asleep…"

"No," he said, "it's not that."

"You could be my true love," she said. "All you got to do is help me and my little girl, give us a chance, love us—that's all you have to do."

"It's not that simple," he said, "there's more to it and you know it just like me." He paused to be sure she grasped all he said or implied. "I'm just not ready—not now," he said, knowing that this had to be his truth.

"Not ready never," she mocked him, moving away from him as far as she could in the small car. Then she went for her purse, and fumbled for a cigarette, throwing the purse on the back seat, and trying time and again to light the cigarette until she simply gave up trying and hit her hand against the window in frustration. He took her cigarette and lit it for her, but when he handed it to her, she opened her window and threw it out.

"I no care," she said, breaking up. "I can live without you and all you men with your love and crazy eyes, and all your *promesas* y *mentiras*—promises and lies."

He started to defend himself, wanting to say he'd neither promised nor lied about anything, but it all seemed too hopeless now.

"You leave me in Tijuana. and I'll soon just be another puta on the street, you leave me and it's all over for me. But I not gonna let you kill me, I don't die a whore in Tijuana. I call up that crazy old couple and fuck with them anywhere they want, I'll go with them—Chicago, New York—and I be their fulltime maid and their fulltime fuck, you wait and see, until someone finds me and knows how to love me, and I get my girl and we live happy, happy!" He drove into the city, turning this way and that and taking her to the block off the Avenida Independencia, where she wanted to get off.

He didn't know what to say. He opened his wallet and gave her all he had. "This is for your girl," his said, hoping it was clear he was not paying her for the night. And with that she reached over as if to give him a kiss but then turned toward the back seat, retrieving her purse. Then she walked in front of his car in the direction of her Tijuana life, so close to beach and border—so close, yet so far from his world. His eyes followed her as she continued down the street getting lost in a sea of heads and faces. He lingered just a moment, and then made his way toward the huge line of traffic; and, turning to see if he had something to drink in the back seat, he saw the money he'd given her in a wad just sitting there. Brooding now in the deepest of funks, he asked himself again if he could do as she asked, and again he realized that no matter what, he could not. He waited his turn as one car and another and still another made it to the border checkpoint. Then, as he crossed over, sadly, reluctantly but oh so finally, he drew out the slip of paper with her number and, to avoid future temptation, threw it out the window just a second before he saw the sign which welcomed him to a place that was indeed his legal country but that could never any longer quite be his home.

And then it occurred to him to ask himself, who was worse? Victor Tapia or he who seemed so nice, he who had decided that he, like Tapia, had to turn his back on María.

La Sefardita

1.

I remember that several years ago when there was a boycott of Austria because an ex-Nazi'd been elected president or some other high position, I broke with the boycott and my own principles. We were in Prague, and who knew if we'd ever get back that way. Surely my little violation wouldn't add up to much, so off we went to Vienna, toured the city, walked the streets, visited the house of Freud, listened to Mozart and Mahler, saw a play by Schnitzler—did all we should do. I even have photos of places we visited, but I honestly can't remember anything about that visit, can't remember a face, a hotel, a palace or any of the other fine places and performances I know we took in. I guess I felt guilty for my lack of solidarity and so I repressed it all—and so I remember nothing about Vienna. All this to say, that I've maybe a similar problem with this story.

To tell the truth, I can only remember the fewest details. I maybe can't tell this story—it's all too vague in my head. I can remember some things that took place long ago in the greatest detail, or so I think, but this one thing remains just too indistinct, too lost. And yet somehow, I want to tell it—somehow, it's a border story I feel I should tell even if I can't bring it fully to life. Somehow, it's important; somehow it says something about her and me, about the times we lived and yes about the border. Maybe it even says something about my sense of Jewish solidarity—and maybe more, I don't know. But I'll try to overcome the memory lapse, I'll try to tell the story, if only to see if I can do it.

2.

First, I can't remember her name. But I once had a Sephardic friend named Margarita, so I guess I'll call her Margarita. I don't remember how I met her, but it must have been at a party or some social event in those wild months after my first marriage. All I know is that I was drawn to her. She was much shorter than even a shrimp like me. She was perhaps too plump, with legs and arms maybe thicker than I liked. She had features of the deepest olive, darker than the usual Mediterranean dark, maybe too dark. But my god, she had the most beautiful face—with almond eyes and the fullest lips, a skin so smooth, her black curly hair cut short, framing her perfectly, making her seem to me like Nefertiti or some other goddess or queen. I remember I couldn't take my eyes off her; and when I finally got up the nerve to talk to her, I was surprised by her seriousness and something rich and deep in her voice. She smiled; I think she joined me in flirting a bit.

Somehow, we got on the subject of our Spanish, and she said she spoke some because she'd lived some time in Spanish North Africa, and Mexico. "Really!" I said and somehow for the first time I saw she was wearing a Jewish star which reached to the cleft between her fine breasts. So here was maybe the first Jewish woman I had met in some time. So beautiful of face, so exotic and still Jewish—this might be the find of my life," I heard myself think. Somehow, we found ourselves suddenly talking in Spanish a bit, but not too well. We laughed and I told her, "Seems to me we both need lessons."

"Maybe so," she agreed, "I've been meaning to do some travel in Mexico to brush up my Spanish, but I haven't had the time or money."

And then I got bold. "Why don't we spend a few hours in Mexico together?" It was spring, and I was ripe for some new adventure and hope. "Why don't I pick you up tomorrow and we'll just drive a way down from the border." So it was that I got her phone number, and the next morning called her, got her address, and went and picked her up.

3.

Well maybe it didn't happen this way. It seems more probable now that I dated her once or twice, took her to a movie, took her to dinner, some more normal things and learned some things about her even as I stole glances at her Jewish star and cleavage, even as I gave her a first kiss and managed at least to brush my hand against the beautiful black hair that curled around and framed her wonderful face.

In my stories I sometimes race too headlong toward the end, fearful I might die before I tell all the stories I have to tell. In this one, where I can remember hardly anything, it seems easy enough to invent short cuts and try racing to the moment of ultimate truth and revelation. So now I'm trying to counter that impulse, slow things down, retard the action to give more weight and gravity to the climax. But of course, you and I know I'm trying to think of how to deal with a story I can't remember, hoping something clicks, catches on and takes off.

So, let's say for now that I didn't race over to her house, and I didn't whisk her away on a first date to Mexico. Let's say I took my good and proper time, getting to know her a little, learning where she went to college, where and what she was now teaching, and learning the story of her family. It seemed her father was a jeweler in Casablanca, where she and her sister were born. But when the Nazis came, the family fled to Ceuta. Some Jewish organization got them to Mexico City, and soon her father was back in business. but none too happy trying to adjust in the city, so when an opportunity came to set up business in Tijuana, he took it, only to have another Jewish organization get them set up in San Diego, where there was no Sephardic synagogue, I think, but he could at least get some religious training for his daughters, at the same time they made their way through the public school system. Once she described to me how she grew up shunned by the Ashkenazi kids around her, how only a few of the boys dared to date her, but how they felt they could take liberties and try to use her as they wouldn't use the other girls, how she stopped dating the Jewish kids and went out with Italians and Mexicans and anyone who wouldn't see her as so exotic and touchable.

Suddenly as she told me all this, I felt very Ashkenazi, very much like one of those kids. Her story made me more tentative, made me keep my distance. Even as I learned all this and saw her a few times and dared to get more intimate in phone calls, I sensed some interior separation, something she wouldn't tell me or maybe something I was feeling without knowing it, something which continued to divide us and maybe had to be overcome or the whole thing would fall apart. Maybe a symptom of this was that we tried to communicate in Spanish as much as we could, as if that somehow neutralized the wall between us, struggling with the language until I probably finally did say, (was it summer now?), "Why don't we go to Rosarito Beach and practice our Spanish?"

4.

So off we went, with her packing a little lunch as if to say, no tacos and no candlelit café with mirrors and flowers. She wore black slacks over her bathing suit and a blouse over her halter. She looked fine and I felt great as we went down across the border and made our way to the beach. The sun was peaking in and out, but it was warm enough. It was a weekday, so there were few people around, just a couple of men hawking beads, boat rides and horseback time.

I spread a towel and she spread out the sandwiches. We talked a little in Spanish, but it became clear that we were both there to explore other things. Somehow this sandy Mexican beach was both our neutral turf and the fulcrum of our possible passion and fruition. I just can't remember all we said and did. I vaguely remember lying on the blanket with her and us talking about how wonderful it would be to just take off and travel all over Mexico and maybe further south. It was all a dream of adventure but one that

78

implied love and maybe marriage, a trip such as my first wife had taught me to value perhaps more than I should have.

But the physical details are all gone. Did she take off her slacks? I think it was too cold and she never did. I know we ate, but did she give me a sandwich, or did she playfully feed it to me flirting and tempting me as she leaned over my body, her Jewish star maybe brushing against my face or my nose? Was it then that I tried to embrace her, because I'm all too sure I must have tried. I can remember kissing her ever so tentatively, trying to hold her against me. Then I can remember her standing and facing the oncoming sunset, with me behind her, my erection aching against her, trying to let her feel it through her clothes—against her bathing suit—no, against her black slacks. I can remember (or do I imagine it?) fondling her breasts as for a moment she turned to kiss me, our lips meeting and my free hand coming to rest on her wonderful hair, until, in the midst of it all, I tasted the salt of tears and felt her heaving and heard her crying even as I held her facing the sea and that declining sun, and sensed her retreat and back away, as if suddenly wounded in the midst of an intimacy she somehow felt impossible to accept.

"*No podemos,*" she whispered, even as she turned to me for a frontal embrace "we can't." And she sobbed and heaved in my arms, as if trusting and maybe even loving me just enough to tell me that nothing would grow of this.

"But why?" I asked her. "I thought it was lovely, I thought we were—"

"It just can't be," she said, "*no puede ser.*" And after sobbing awhile, she withdrew from me, and started gathering up our things, with me helping, dutifully getting everything in the car, driving back toward the border and waiting over an interminable hour in line. Then came the quick ride back to her place—all this time hardly saying a word, with her seeking Spanish music stations, us listening to bolero after bolero, but no longer as part of any ritual of seduction.

When we arrived at her house, she sought to get out with only a thank you. And when I said I'd call her, she said ok but I knew she meant no.

"Tell me," I almost asked her, "what happened." But as I remember, I didn't ask her, perhaps because I already knew or perhaps because I too knew we could go nowhere. At least that's what I think I thought at the time and if this were so, I must've felt a flush of shame. The only thing I know for sure, I think, is I never called her again. That much I remember.

The Daughters of Sánchez

At a certain point in his eternal quest for women, Mel found himself frequenting a Mexican bar not too far from the center of San Diego but adjacent to the freeway that went down to the border.

Mel certainly knew the etiquette for a white man entering such a bar, just as Black friends had taught him how to enter one of their watering holes. When you come in, you look no one in the eye. After you're frisked, you take your seat at the bar if you can or at a table toward the rear, if there's one available. But even approaching your seat, you look at no one, and you certainly don't stare. At best you should look at edge of the bar or the edge of the table you're being assigned to. When you sit down, you ask for a drink as soon as possible, looking past your server, he or she, at the mirror or a window or a poster or sign on the wall; or, if there's a pool game in session, you can look at the game—but not at the players. What you never want to do is be found looking directly or for long at any one and certainly not at a woman. Only gradually, drink in hand, can you slowly look over the scene—see if there are other gringos, first of all, and get a sense of how rough or tough the place is that you've entered. If it seems too tough, consider leaving but slowly, nonchalantly, as if nothing mattered at all. If it doesn't seem too tough and you decide to stay, you should wish yourself good luck, hope you've sized things up properly, and hope you get through the night.

In this bar, Mel had the best luck of all. The person responsible for waiting on him was a cute and friendly *mexicana* whose job was indeed to talk and flirt with her male customers. This one was special because she just started talking to him in the most easy and sprightly way, and in English. But when she heard Mel speak his primitive but improving Spanish, she started right off talking to him in *mexicano,* asking him where he was from, and when finding out he was a pure gringo, she complemented him on

81

his Spanish and said, "You must know lots of Mexican girls to speak so good."

"Well, yes," he admitted. "I've been working on it."

"Well now you know another one without having to work at all," she said, smiling and doing everything in her power to make him feel at home in a bar that otherwise seemed to have enough rough edges for him to consider making a quick exit.

"Do you think I'm safe here?" he asked her up front. "Because I sure don't want to be where I'm making people unhappy and maybe angry."

No, *cielo* (she literally called him *heaven*), don't worry about it. If anyone gets smart with you, they'll have to deal with me and the other bargirls. Looking around, he indeed noticed the other girls, all good looking, and a little tough looking, like Ringo Starr's *chola* sisters in the movie version of Terry Southern's *Candy*.

So, she made him feel safe, and she made him admire her for the way she handled him and others in the bar. And her swell looks had him eating out of her hand like the squirrel of his sweetest dreams. He tried not to talk to her too much and spent most of his time watching the couples that wandered on to the floor to dance cumbia and polka. He tried to pick up on the steps, but he certainly didn't ask anyone to dance, when it dawned on him that the waitresses were supposed to get the customers going, to keep them in a festive and drinking mood, he figured. But who should come and choose him as if he were her Mexican boyfriend? Of course, he couldn't refuse, though his dancing was just awful, and he stepped on her toes time and again. But she was such a good sport laughing away. And Mel had a fine time, dancing with her and starting to launch another fantasy of another wondrous affair. He even went so far as to ask for her name. "Brisela," she answered, "What's yours?" And he told her his name, but not what he did for a living or anything else that he feared might turn her off.

Later in the evening, when things were winding down, Mel dared to ask Brisela if she wanted a lift, to which she said no thanks, she had a ride; but if he wanted to hang out with her and her friends, they were going to hook up at an all-night restaurant not too far away. Mel wondered if this were a good idea, but how could he pass up such an open invitation which offered him entry into a world he might otherwise never know—a world that might even enable him to grasp the lay of the land for his possible future life? So he left the bar and drove to the restaurant, parking his car in the adjacent lot and waiting a while for at least some of the others from the bar to park and enter the place before exiting his car and opening the restaurant front door.

He looked for her and then spotted a long table filled with many people, some of whom he recognized as waitresses, waiters, bartenders, and clients from the bar. Virtually all of them seemed to be Mexican, but Mel relaxed when he spotted Brisela seated with the group. "Hola Brisela, hola todos!" he managed to say.

"Here's my dancing partner," Brisela said, and she introduced him all around to the group, asking him first to remind her of his name. He was perhaps more worried about class than race because this looked like almost a purely working-class crowd. But nobody asked him what he did, but what he wanted to eat, and he ordered apple pie à la mode and coffee, and just listened as one person or another launched an anecdote about one person or another at least some members of the group knew about.

Then curiously, they started telling border stories, about how this one got across and that one went back only to cross again, how some smart border-crosser fooled a *coyote* or la *migra* or whoever, how this one married a *gabacha*—you know, a white girl— or a Chicana or whatever.

"One of the biggest problems of this hick town," said one of the men, "is that it just doesn't attract enough Chicana women. That's what *nosotros los mexicanos* need—more Spanish-speaking Chicana women so we can all straighten out our papers."

Everyone lifted their glasses to drink their cokes and coffees to that. But then another *mexicano* said that that was no good, because the Chicana women were too *brava* and fiery and didn't respect men. It would all be so easy if they were *mansas*, you know, *suaves*—smooth, submissive," he said, "but they're not. The gringas'll divorce you in a flash, but the Chicana women will leave you and take off for L.A. before you get your pants back on."

Everyone laughed again, as the speaker finished his rap.

"No, the best are the *mexicanas*," he said, "even when they can't help with a single paper."

"They're the best and it's a good thing that most of us are stuck with 'em!"

"The trouble is," said one of the *mexicanas*, "that you guys want your Mexican wives, but you also want your girlfriends on the side—and they can be anything, even *mexicana*, chicana, or maybe even gringa, as long as they give you what you want."

And now Mel realized that all the women were indeed Mexican and they now called out "Amen" and it was now they who toasted.

"Well, I may be married but I ain't castrated," said one of the men.

"Maybe this'll be your lucky night," said one of the girls, as the others laughed. "All right you guys, raise your hands if you're married—be honest now, let's see what kind of cards we got in this deck."

Virtually no hands went up. "My god," said another girl. "All you guys can't be liars. Though looking at you, man, I can see that no woman'd want you"

"My god, look at this one, you can even see where he usually wears his ring."

"And this one has the face of one brow-beaten mother-fucker!"

"And this one, looks like he's been sucking on pussy with his dick hanging in the wind!"

Pretty soon, everyone was howling as the women went around the table spotting each male.

Finally, they came to Mel, and he held his breath. "And what about you, newcomer? You enjoying yourself listening to us make fun of each other while you're looking at Brisela and wanting to eat her up like she's a piece of chocolate cake."

"Cause she's a hot brown babe," said one of the others, "with a big fat Mexican ass."

Again they all laughed except the woman who was sitting at Brisela's side, who told them to can it. "Leave the dude alone," she said. "This guy doesn't even know who and what he's dealing with."

"Well, he seems a fair enough dude to me," said another.

"And you speak some mean Mexican," his friend said.

"Well what about it, buddy, you married or what?"

"Divorced," he said, but again looking no one in the eye.

"Looking in Mexican bars," said another, challenging him a bit.

"Bueno a mi me gustan a los mexicanos," he said.

'You mean you like the *mexicanas*," said his defender now probing a bit. "'Cause you don't look like the kinda guy who'd come in looking for one of us guys." And everyone laughed again.

"Wouldn't mind having some Mexican friends," he offered, realizing that he really had never had a male Mexican friend.

"What, you wanna get buddy-buddy with us and then steal our women?" said one of the guys.

"All right," said Brisela, "Let the guy be, he's just here being social."

"Just a lonely divorcee looking for some *mexicana* action," said another guy.

"Hell," said still another, "I'd marry him if he could straighten out my papers!"

And with that everyone laughed again. On the bantering went but without any real sense of threat. And soon they tired of interrogating him and started drifting off in their own directions. Eventually they started to leave—the obvious couples going their way, and the singles, married or not, going theirs. Mel said good night to everyone, trying to get and remember some of the names.

Pretty soon, it was down to Brisela and the woman sitting at her side. And almost immediately Mel understood the situation, as he just observed something masculine in the friend's demeanor. "So now," said the woman, "you get the picture, right?"

"Yes, I guess I do."

"I don't hold it against you, and I'll tell you what, if you want, we can even be friends, you know, hang out together if you want, maybe go over to TJ and dance and stuff."

"That would be great," he said.

"What do you say?" said the woman to Brisela.

And Brisela answered with a frankness that surprised him and maybe her friend. "Look, he's a sweet guy," she said, "and he's really sweet on me, so I don't have anything against him hanging out with us or anything—it would be fine with me and maybe some fun, feeling him all hot for me and almost dying 'cause he'd have to keep his hands to himself."

"Sounds fine with me," said her friend, shaking his hand, and surprisingly giving him a hug.

"So where do you wanna go tomorrow?" she said, "Cause we're off tomorrow and we're ready to go."

"I don't know," he said at a loss and not knowing what to make of this talking and arranging. "I guess we can go out and chase girls together," he said.

And the two women started to laugh. "Mexican girls!" exclaimed the friend, starting to crack up.

"Mexican girls!" he repeated.

And then Brisela kissed him and the woman kissed Brisela and even gave him a little kiss. He felt he was having some hint of heaven as Brisela gave him her telephone number just when they were moving toward the door and going toward their cars.

It was so good, he thought, imagining his fun day with the two girls drinking their way from bar to bar and adventure to adventure. *So good, maybe too good,* he mused. And when he tried to call them the next morning, he was terribly disappointed though not so surprised when he found that the telephone number Brisela'd given him somehow didn't work.

And when 9 p.m. came and he could return to the bar to see if they'd show up, he got ready to go, but then sat down in his chair ready to spend another miserable night alone. "Y ¿que esperaste? pendejo" he heard himself call himself an idiot in Spanish—which was surely a kind of minimal triumph in the midst of it all.

Flora Ruvalcaba

1.

"Flora, Flora Ruvalcaba," Mel said, fascinated with the sound; "Flora Ruvalcaba," "Flora como una flor, … like a flower. Flora y fauna, Flor y fierra," "Beauty and the beast," he laughed, looking in the mirror. La bella flor de mis sueños," he whispered, "The lovely flower of my dreams." "Flor de mi alma—my soul, Flor de mi corazón—my heart."

He had just met her some days before at a party, and ever since was trying to get up the nerve to call her. His friend Roy Johnson told him not to call right away. "Get a woman wondering if you're gonna call, wait until you've almost busted a gut with the waiting, until you're past the point where you can't stand it."

Roy was his key strategist at how to pursue and get women. He was often right, but this time Mel was not so sure. Roy did not mess with Latina women; Black himself, he lived the search for white women that was the norm for black men in those tense and historic days. He lived in a border city where a sea of Latinos was almost invisible to the Black and white world of his imagination.

"One thing is the Mexican ladies," Roy said. "They can look just fine—fabulous even, and they might fall for you, or at least make you think so if you got money and a passport. But those Chicana bitches—you can date them at your own peril—they might be beautiful, but they're hard as nails, and hard to get in the sack. They're so damn Catholic with you and end up with big bellies when you're not looking. They might give you some game if you try hard enough, but in the end, they only really go with their own. And here's the worst of it. You can treat 'em nice, very nice. But they'll drop you in a minute for some Mexican guy who treats them like shit, and beats 'em on Saturday night."

Mel was just tired of hearing all this. Recuperating all too slowly from his first marriage, he found himself turning to Mexican women, to music on the Spanish-speaking stations, listening to the announcers and songs. learning who the singers were, the styles, the key types of melodramas portrayed. "Sombras nada más!—Nothing but shadows" he sang along with the radio, committing treason against his once deep Sinatra roots. Now, after some initial failed encounters, he had met Flora; and though he knew she wasn't a normal kind of beautiful, he found her so. He loved the low notes of her voice, the page boy cut of her hair, the dark olive hue of her skin, the serious and dramatic look in her eyes, even the slightness of her form, her small rump, her skinny and slightly bowed legs.

"Don't ask me out," she said. "I know you want to, but don't call me," she said, daring hm. Mel didn't even know who hosted this party. He had gone there with a friend and hardly knew a soul in the place. How did he even start to talk to a woman who attracted him so? He would usually shy away. He had no decent small talk, and his dancing was appalling—a sure ticket to thank you and goodbye (and yet Roy told him, "if you want a Latina, you got to dance."). There was no way he could even think of breaking the ice.

"You're a professor, right?" she said to him as he poured himself a drink.

"What makes you think so?" he asked. She took the drink from him, as if he had offered it, and stirred it with her forefinger.

"You look like one," she said.

"And how does a professor look?"

"Shoes unshined, laces almost undone, glasses—dirty ones at that, sloppy old jacket, $10 haircut, funny Jewish face—you're a typical youngish Jewish professor type, you probably teach literature and are a big hit with your white, blonde and blue-eyed girl students, who think you're the nicest, funniest guy. Should I go on?" she dared, drinking the drink.

89

"No need, Sherlock Holmes," he said pouring himself one again.

"If I were in your class, you'd give me an A," she said.

"Why?"

"Because you'd forget about those other girls. You'd look into my dark eyes, and you'd be dying to go to bed with me."

"What makes you think so?" he said.

"It's written all over your face," she said, and it was true, he knew, and had been true probably even before she took the drink from his hand.

"And would I have any luck?" he asked.

"First give me the A and then you'll find out."

"But how can I give you an A if you aren't in my class?"

"That's for you to figure out," she said, downing the rest of her drink. "But I'll tell you one thing: we'll never be in the same class."

She started to leave, as if the whole encounter or test had come to an end, and she, not he, was passing out the grades. She laughed as he quickly reached for a piece of paper and a pen he had in his pocket. "I'm Mel," he said.

"Mel," she repeated laughing, "Like Melba Toast a little overdone and crumby!" she all but chortled. "I'm Flora Ruvalcaba," she said, with her deep, wondrous voice. "Let's see if you can even pronounce it."

"Flora … Ruvalcaba," he said, trying to get the authentic sound for each syllable.

90

"Very good," she said. "B-plus—and now you'll never be able to get me out of your mind." With that, she wrote down a series of numbers. "Don't worry," she said, "it's my real number. But that doesn't mean you're getting anywhere."

"That's understood," he said. "Eso se entiende."

"Ah," she said, "Good try. Buenas noches," she said, "I have to go." And go she did.

2.

Now he could follow Roy's advice no longer; he could resist no further. It was Saturday morning, more than a week after he'd met her, and he had to speak to her and see where this might lead. He had been thinking of her so much, he'd neglected the woman he was dating and sleeping with—nothing else seemed to matter. So he called, and she answered.

"Flora," he said, not having a clue what to say.

"Ah," she said, "it's you."

"Yes," he answered, in no way sure she knew it was him.

"I guess you held out as long as you could, to show me I wasn't so important. But I knew I was, I knew you'd have to call."

"And how did you know all that?"

"Because of the way you said my name and because I'm irresistible—especially to a vulnerable man like you."

He was speechless, "You're right, right as you always seem to be."

"Listen," she said, "I was born and raised here, my parents are from Mexico, but here for years. I'm not a college girl like your pretty, white girl students, I went to community college. I work in a little social service office for Latinos mainly, I have a little boy, José, I'm recently divorced, resentful of men (what woman isn't?),

91

and I've never gone out with a *gabacho*—a gringo, let alone a Jewish one. So I'm not the romantic woman you're going crazy about. And by the way, I only speak a little Spanish, so don't think you're going to improve your language skills by dating me so you can go after all the border señoritas of your white boy wet dreams."

"I want to see you," he said.

"When?" she said.

"As soon as possible."

"All right," she said. "Where are you going to take me?"

"Let's run away to Mexico," he blurted out.

"I knew you were going to say that," she said. "You're so obvious."

"We could go to China for all I care, but Mexico's closer," he answered.

"All right," she said, "My ex will pick up José soon, so you can kidnap me around 6, and take your señorita to dinner como Dios manda—as God so wills," she said.

"What?" he said.

"Nothing," she said, laughing, and hung up.

He called again. "You forgot to give me your address," he said.

"Did I?" she said, laughing again.

3.

Her door was open, with just a screen door in front of it. He rang the bell and she called, "Come on in, I'm almost ready."

He waited in the living room examining pictures of parents, sisters, and brothers, maybe her son, but no one looking like he might be the ex-husband. Out she came, looking so wonderful with

92

her black hair and olive glow, the red of her lipstick, bright and alluring, she so svelte and lovely.

"I know," she said, "I look like your dream come true," she laughed, and then she proceeded to identify the people in the pictures. Soon they were out the door, driving past downtown and him opting for the route across the bay over the Coronado bridge, to the town and its well-known Victorian hotel, heading for Imperial Beach and the border.

"Let's stop for a drink," he suggested, and he pulled up to the hotel.

They had margaritas and watched the sun set over the water, she looking down toward the south and the border dust. "So different here, from the life over there," she said with some bitterness.

"Yes," he said grimly, "hard to believe we're so close and yet so far and away…"

"You said it, and not me," she said.

"I didn't mean us," he insisted,

"Didn't you?" she said, finishing her drink.

Of course, it was a mistake to take her to Tijuana, but he felt compelled. In recent months, he had explored the city, trying to escape the prostitute zones, the bar scene, the painted burros, and find where the people lived their Mexican, border lives. He drove her around to Parque Libertad, and then headed down to a fine Italian restaurant out along the road toward Rosarito.

"Some other time, we could go and stay in Ensenada," he said.

"You mean when we're lovers, right?"

"Yes," he had to admit.

"Don't dream so much, live in the moment—seize the day," she said, getting out of the car. They shared a bottle of wine and a rich meal, speaking some broken Spanish to the waiter and host. Everything seemed so right, so perfect.

"Now where are you going to take me?" she asked, "What terrible plan do you have?"

"Have you ever been to the Foreign club?" he asked. "It's right on Avenida Revolución but it's different," he said. "No prostitutes, just a place where the Mexicans go to hear some music and dance."

He drove along the main tourist strip and parked the car, taking her arm, feeling wonderful, as they walked some, and entered a kind of patio, where, tucked in the corner, was the sign reading "Foreign Club" and "Bien Venidos." True to his words, the place was a respectable dancing club, with many young Tijuana middle class men and women, sitting in groups, often with family members around endless tables, listening first to a fine guitarist and then a jazz group, and then finally a trio playing old-style, romantic boleros, including a few he had learned to sing. He danced with her, with his usual insecurity but insistent on establishing himself as one who would bring her to the dance floor.

"You're not as terrible as I thought you'd be," she said, almost smiling.

"But still pretty bad—malo," he said.

"Horrible, de verdad—to tell the truth!" she said, and he winced, but then joined her soft laughter.

"We have to go," she said a small time later. "A big family day tomorrow—and I have to do the cooking."

They walked to the parking lot, and when he opened the car door to let her go by, she looked at him and kissed him on the lips; and when he entered, he kissed her, soon meeting her tongue as they explored each other's mouths. Waiting at the border, they kissed a few times again; crossing, they drove into San Diego and over to her apartment further north, holding hands.

"Well, profé, you did pretty good taking your Mexican girl back to Mexico, showing her around like a tour guide and taking her to the one place where all the *mexicanas* can look down their noses at a Mexican American girl," she said, smiling. "But don't worry, let's see what you can cook up next time." He kissed her as he left her at the door. "Give me your number," she said. "I'll call you," she said writing it down, "But don't expect me to call tomorrow." She kissed him on the cheek. "It wasn't as bad as I thought it would be," she said. "But it was pretty *horrible* anyway!"

4.

That very next evening she called him, with him preparing his classes but waiting by the phone. "How did the family party go?" he asked.

"Don't even go there," she said, "I'm exhausted. But come on over."

In a rush, he was in his car and off, making only one short stop on the way and reaching her place with ease this time. She came to the door, a transformed woman in levi pants and a white blouse, open at the neck. He kissed her right away and gave her the rose he'd purchased. "Una flor—a flower— for Flora," she said, kissing him and savoring the rose. "Not so bad, Mr. profc."

She gestured for him to sit on the couch where she had been watching TV, apparently drinking from the wine glass on the table in front of the couch. He sat watching dumbly as she put the flower in a stem glass and then took a drink of the wine. She offered him some of it, and he could not resist drinking from her glass. Then she sat down and watched the screen with him for a second, only to then turn her face toward him and kiss him, letting out the smallest moan as she kissed him again. Soon her head was in his lap, staring up at him as he bent over and stared back at her, deep into her deep eyes, feeling his passion for her rise and kissing her again. Then she sat up again and embraced him, pressing herself against him, kissing him harder this time, kissing him one time and then another and another. Soon they were kissing with greater force, his tongue exploring her mouth like Columbus discovering an ancient but somehow new world, like Cortez entering Tenochtitlán, with her breathing hard with each discovery and making a few finds of her own, conquering him as she led his hands to her small breasts, helping him unbutton her blouse.

Then she got up. "Not here," she said, "Come over here,' and she led him into the bedroom. She took off her blouse, and he saw her small and lovely breasts in her bra; he took her in his arms and kissed her again, reaching down toward her breasts, opening her bra and then kissing and yes, sucking on her nipples. Everything was moving in a terrible, exciting rush, when the phone rang and she suddenly got up, answering. "All right," she said, hanging up. "I'm sorry," she said, "but you have to go. My ex is bringing José home early, and you don't want to be here when they drive up."

He felt breathless, horrendous from the interruption. "I can't believe this has happened," he said.

"I feel terrible too, but this is what happens when you have kids. But don't worry, we'll get together soon, you know we will, right?"

"Yes," he said, "of course. This has to be, you and me."

"Yes," she said, lightening up, "this is my new life adventure."

And off he went, frustrated but hopeful that his understanding would pay him dividends in a romance that would begin to flourish.

5.

Mel waited a few days hoping she would call. But finally he could wait no longer; and as another dreaded weekend approached, he called her.

"You shouldn't have called," she said. "You should have waited."

"I couldn't," he said. "I was afraid you wouldn't call."

"You need to have more confidence and more patience."

He didn't know what to say, and then they both spoke at the same time. "What?" she asked.

"Nothing," he said miserably, "whatever you say."

"Look, things are more complicated than you think," she said. "Give me your work number."

He gave it, growing more miserable even as his hopes persisted.

"I'll call you," she said, "but don't call me."

The days passed, and it only got worse. He didn't know what to make of what had happened. Had her ex got wind of some new relationship about to begin? Did he have the house bugged? Was their son spying for him? Had he moved back in? And meanwhile the silence persisted, as he waited for a call to his office he knew might not indeed come. In fact, he got tired of waiting in his office and went defiantly to the cafeteria, trying to prove his independence to himself, but knowing also that if he didn't answer, the call would relay to the secretary who would tell him when he returned. Each day he waited, and no call came. He knew the symptoms and where this might lead, but he felt paralyzed. Each day after his classes, he held his office hours, and waited. After those hours, he went to the cafeteria and then returned to the office. Each day there was no word from the secretary, and he would make his way to home. On it went for several days, when finally, one day, returning from the cafeteria at 4, he answered the ringing phone and found her on the line.

"So, I found you at last," she said, "Why have you been avoiding me?" He was astounded and speechless. "I've called you almost every day," she said.

"But I didn't get any messages."

"I didn't leave any. That's not me."

"Flora, when can I see you?"

"You can't. Not now, maybe someday soon," she said.

"Tell me, Flora, what's going on?"

"Nothing's going on. Does something always have to be going on? We can talk, at least a little. That's something, isn't it? That's all I can give you right now."

"You're back with your husband," he suggested.

"No."

"Your son doesn't want you dating," he offered.

"No," she said. "Nothing like that." There was a big pause and she said, "How are you?"

"Miserable," he answered.

"Don't feel bad, go to a movie, take out one of your little white girlfriends."

"I only want to see you."

"I know," she said, "And you can't, *pobrecito*—poor boy."

"You're mocking me," he accused her. "No, I'm commiserating with you. You think I don't know what it's like not seeing the one you're stuck on?"

"And you're not stuck on me."

"I didn't say that," she said. "I miss you."

"But you hardly know me."

"I miss getting to know you— it was going so well."

"Don't remind me," he said.

"You keep good," she said, and she hung up.

The next day, he was in his office at four once again and again she called. "What are you doing?" she asked.

"Nothing, grading papers. Waiting to see if you'd call."

"Are you giving out any A's?"

"No," he said, suffering through it.

"What are you thinking about?"

"You," he said, "no one but you."

"Que lindo," she said.

"Que linda tú," he replied.

"Me tengo que ir—gotta go."

"Don't go, talk to me."

"Mañana," she said, hanging up.

But mañana was Saturday, and she wouldn't be calling. Roy called him up and invited him to a party. He went, flirted as much as he could get himself to do. But to no avail.

"You gotta get over this," Roy said. "When you don't got one, you gots to get another," he added, imitating the most stereotyped ghetto talk. But he couldn't even think of it, he felt trapped in a nightmare—terrified but not wanting to wake up. The weekend came and went, and his depression grew. Monday came and he made it to four o'clock. She called on the dot. But it was more of the same: both tempting and discouraging, giving him hope only to dash him down. Always that low deeply intimate voice, as if they'd been lovers for years, and she never once called him by name—somehow it was more intimate that way. You didn't have to say the name of your love when you woke up, names didn't count, only the nameless intimacy of it all, as if soul could touch soul without any word intervening. But she of course had a name, that beautiful name that made him think of flowers and perfume and precious stones that glowed like the warmest embers in the heart of the heartless world of his life—warm and shining precious embers, burning like a rose in his thorn-torn *corazón*.

Each day she called at four and each day he was tempted not to answer, but always gave in, panicking to answer before she hung up. She immediately sensed his game and mocked him. "I know what you're doing, I know you're trying not to answer, but then you do, you're trying to show you don't care but you do. 'Don't you know little fool, you never can win, Use your mentality, step up to reality,'" she sang, shocking him that this beautiful Chicana woman knew the inner structure of his New Jersey, Sinatra-driven passion—Cole Porter as much as Gershwin.

And he knew she had him, knew she'd shaped his passion into a heart she could pierce with the arrows of her whims and inspirations. He felt defenseless, totally victimized, shipwrecked on the rocks of his constructed fantasies and hopes. Each day she called and pressured the arrow into different recesses of his wound, breaking down the fiber, the membranes until he could barely breathe or live. And yet, he loved the sweet ache of the incessant pain she inflicted, waited each day to receive more, terrified that she might not call him—and then what would he do?

And of course, she began to turn erratic, calling five before or five or ten after four, or not calling one day, but calling the next as if nothing had happened, and then not calling two days, then three, then calling again, as if testing him every way, as if waiting and wanting him to say, "You know what? You've been playing long enough, I think it's about time you stopped calling." And indeed he thought of it; indeed, he felt he had to do it; there was no future in any of this. The only way he had to save a little of his pride was to do just this: break with her calls, break with his addiction to his Floral needs, his Ruvalcaba dreams.

But he could not just do it, he had to have one last conversation. And so when she called him, he told her. "Listen this can't go on. I need to see you soon. You name where and when, but I have to see you."

"You can't," she said. "I can't see you."

"Then I won't answer the phone," he said. "This is the last phone call."

"I don't believe you," she said. "You can't resist."

"Look, I don't even remember what you look like," he lied.

"That's not true," she said. "You know I'm pretty, you know you want to kiss me and hold me. You know I have skinny legs and I should be broader, but nothing matters because you want to be with me so much you're dying inside."

"Yes," he said, alright," he said. "But I'm not the total coward you take me for. If you're not going to see me, I'm going to break off this phone romance."

"You love this romance just as it is, or you'd do something about it," she said defiantly.

"What do you mean?" he asked, taken aback.

"I mean if you wanted to see me so bad, why didn't you just call me up and tell me you're coming over, do something a man would do and not a timid mouse like you."

"All right," he said, calling her bluff. "I'm coming to see you tonight."

101

"You can't," she said.

"Why not?" he answered.

"Because I have another date, if you must know."

"Then why are you egging me on?"

"I don't know. I can't explain it. Maybe because I hate, maybe because I love, maybe because I hate you for making me love you a little"

"Let's go out tomorrow," he said, totally confused by her but trying not to drown. "All right," she said, "call me," she said, hanging up.

He called her the next afternoon and asked her about her date. "I didn't go out," she admitted or lied. "I was lying to you."

"Will you go out with me tonight?"

"Yes, but late. Call me about nine."

He called again at nine sharp.

"I can't go out with you," she said.

"Why not?"

"I just can't. I don't know why," she cried. "Don't even bother to ask," and she was indeed sobbing over the phone.

"Let me come by and talk to you," he said like a boxer who's taken it on the chin but still wants to keep fighting.

"No," she said.

"I'm coming by," he said.

"If you do, I'm going to call the police."

"What?"

"I'm not fooling," she said. "You try to break in my house and the police will be right on you."

"You know I'm not breaking in, you can't mean it," he said.

"Try me," she answered.

He had to go, and so he went. He drove over to her neighborhood up on a mesa, and turned onto the street where she lived, and sure enough, he saw the lights of a police car right in front of her house.

6.

He made a U-urn in a driveway and went the other way, driving out of the neighborhood, onto the freeway, not knowing where to go on this oh-so-sweet San Diego night. The humiliation he felt was immense. She had turned him into a predator, a stalker— she had criminalized his feelings for her. He had never felt so brought down, so divested, bested and all but busted .

"Where else can I go?" he thought, "where does a rejected lover go?"

So he headed south, but avoided the Coronado bridge turnoff and shot straight past National City, Chula Vista and San Ysidro, crossing the border and finding his way not to the elegant Italian Restaurant nor the fine Foreign club, nor even the night madness of Avenida Revolución, but to the Zona Norte red light district known to all the lonely hearts of San Diego. He walked in and out of different bars, sampling different drinks, propositioned by different prostitutes. But he couldn't go with any of them, couldn't sit still. The night wore on, and he staggered back toward his car. "Papi," called a prostitute from a doorway, with a voice that sounded strangely like Flora's. "*Ven conmigo, Papi*—come with me, sweetie," she said sweetly. And he couldn't resist any longer but entered her house. "Only 20, papi," she told him, and he took out his wallet to get the business part of things done. She was not bad looking, he observed—lighter than Flora's dark-lovely, thinner than Flora, not as beautiful but far from ugly. "*Vente aquí,* —come here, Papi," she said, making him at home, lying next to him caressing him, rubbing her breasts against him, smiling, and unzipping his fly. She stroked him as she smiled, feigning kisses and he couldn't help but feel aroused. "*Me quieres coger*—you wanna fuck me, Papi?"

"*Sí,"* he said, and she kissed his cheek and lured him, until he indeed began undressing her, making love to her.

"*Soy un muchacho*," she said quickly,

"What?" he said.

"I'm a boy, y quiero hacerte feliz, I wanna make you happy, pero no puedo esta noche, I can't tonight, *papi; he follado demasiado ya*—I've fucked too much already." And suddenly it was clear to him, his erection and interest abating.

"I sorry, Papi. You no like boys?"

"I don't think so," he said, "At least not tonight—maybe some other time," he said, making his way out onto the street and into his car, with no one to kiss him and give him hope as he waited his turn in the long line of cars seeking to cross the border.

Then he made it home and to bed, crying with frustration and bitterness at his experience—so much passion and pain to end in the arms of one he felt was a travesty of a woman, his Mexican romance clearly over, at least for now.

7.

How many days and weeks passed before Mel felt relatively recovered? Flora and all that had happened began to fade in his memory a bit, when Roy apparently felt he had to tell him that a friend of his had talked to him about Flora, that he had dated her and pretty rapidly bedded her, and she'd told him some funny stories about a guy she'd dated who seemed to have the same name as Roy's friend Mel and who just didn't know how to click with her. His friend told him Flora was eager to continue their affair, but he decided against it. "'A pretty skinny bitch,' he said. 'And really nothing special. Working class barrio girl and her brother's a cop—

104

that's what really cooled it for me. And I just didn't like the way she talked about your friend.' It's like I told you," Roy said, "you can't trust those Chicana girls. I tried to warn you, but some guys are too crazy to listen."

Mel could only nod his assent as he went about his lonely life. She would have soon become a passing memory. But one night he and his roommate threw one of the wild parties they were known for—a blast with all kinds of people showing up at all hours. And then, who should arrive but Flora Ruvalcaba on the arm of Roy's cousin Roland. How could she just show up like this at his own house, after throwing him for a loop and making light of all she had put him through and now coming to where he lived, coming to his haunt to flaunt a new love in front of him and his friends. At first, he tried to hide his feelings but then hearing her laughter and having taken one drink too many, he felt the need to confront her. Finding her alone on the front porch, he came up to her and started to talk. He tried to speak lightly but it just didn't work. Finally, he let loose what he felt.

"How can you be such a bitch and do this—come to my house after manipulating me, calling the police on me and then making fun of me with people sure to tell me?"

"I don't know," she said, "I've tried to figure it out, but it's beyond me. Maybe it's because Jews exploit Mexican women on the job, maybe because they own Mexico, maybe because you think you're a kind of Conquistador and I'm your Malinche, maybe it's because you killed Christ and now want to kill us too. Maybe it's because I owe it to the Vírgen de Guadalupe. Maybe it's because I've been hurt and want revenge. Maybe it's because you, you're so ready to be my victim, even though I might care for you somewhere inside me."

And then, strangely, she kissed him, pressed her body against him and then was gone—not even looking for Roland's cousin, just running up the stairs and gone from his life, just as suddenly as she had entered it.

Afterwards, Mel recovered, and struggled on, but he could never quite get the sound of her name out of his head and sometimes, even years later, he would even hear her whisper to him in his dreams: "Flora, Flora Ruvalcaba."

Two Nights of Tlatelolco

1.

Lonnie Hart, an African American social work grad student at San Diego State, had become my bridge friend from the breakup of my first marriage and almost to the start of my second. I tried to make a new single life, but I went from disaster to disaster, unable to do much of anything, teaching my classes minimally, racing from campus toward one pickup bar or another, driven, I guess, by post-marital depression and desperation. In the meantime, I did try to write new plays I couldn't get together for production, tried to write stories I couldn't finish—so that, stymied in every way, I found myself bedding the wrong women, drinking too much, spending much of my little spare money on shrinks who tried to put my head together and expending hours in traffic court dealing with my drunk driving.

At the same time, Lonnie chose another path, getting close to a young Irish girl named Karen, cultivating the relationship until gradually over time, they grew together and consummated what was now a deepened and seasoned love. As this happened, Lonnie got more and more unhappy with my erratic and wayward ways, my obsessive lusts and flings, my agonizing discontents that were disturbing his love affair and his girl. Lonnie was really alarmed. Too many strange women—hookers and waifs—seemed to be passing through the house, too much noise was coming from the bedroom which was too close to the happy couple.

"You can't go on like this," he told me. "It's so sad to see someone with your talents just throwing your life away, hitting on every woman friend who passes by and screwing everything up. And now Karen's getting upset because she cares for you but hates what you're doing."

"I can't help it," I answered. "I want to live, but don't know how."

Then, in the summer of 1968, as the production of my first play in years failed to jell and we cancelled the production, I went over to the house of my star actor friend to talk things over, only to see Bobby Kennedy get shot on the TV set. We sat awhile, stunned, watching the news coverage, both broken from the collapse of the production and now the death of political hopes we shared, finally saying goodbye with me returning home, totally lost.

"I can't stand it," I told Lonnie, "I've gotta get out of here, I've got to go to Mexico, and I want you to go with me."

"But I can't," Lonnie protested.

"I can't go alone," I repeated, "and you're the only one who can help me."

"But what about Karen? My relationship's just getting there."

"Tell her you need to help me, that I'm on the verge of a breakdown. Tell her you love her, and you'll marry her or do whatever she wants when you come back. Tell her anything—this'll be the trip of your life—it's going to be your great adventure before marriage."

Strangely enough Lonnie agreed, maybe fearful for me. "I can't let him go alone," he must've told Karen. And she must have agreed to take care of their new dog, which took up half the house. "Maybe we'll get a chance to think about where we're at and what we want to do," maybe she or he said... So, within a few days, we were on their way across the border.

2.

Nothing seemed to go right. The plan was to drive to Mexicali and then down past Mazatlán and Guadalajara, Michoacán, and Guanajuato before heading toward D.F. and then

Acapulco and who knew where else. But just past the Sonoita checkpoint, in Santa Ana, Sonora, the car broke down, and they had to leave it behind awaiting parts that would come the following week, while they worked their way down toward Guadalajara on the bus. The only half-guarantee for the money advanced and the car to be fixed was the fact that the mechanic was a fervent Seven Day Adventist.

Down they went to Hermosillo, then Guaymas. But the trip was tedious by bus. They found a cheap hotel in Mazatlán and beached it a few days, hitting the local bars, at Mel's insistence, each night. Mel tried to pick up on the girls, but he was so tense and eager, and incapable of small talk, that he had no success. Better looking than his friend, even-tempered, with the sweetest demeanor, Lonnie was less inclined to pursue any women, though he was friendly and open, so that the few women they talked to gravitated toward him. Mel was quite unhappy with his failures, so they bussed it to Tepic and San Blas, where, after checking into a rundown hotel, he insisted they go on a jungle boat road late in the day. It turned out to be so late that the boatman got nervous as the dark came on and the jungle creatures carried on their mad and noisy hunt for food. It was clear the boatman was getting very edgy, swinging his weak battery lamp this way and that.

"I think we're in trouble," said Lonnie. "If this is how he makes a living and this is his turf, and he's scared, then we should be really panicking."

Mel spoke his improving Spanish to the boatman, "Why did you take us so far if you knew it was getting dark in no time?"

"Because you wanted to go," he said, "And I needed the money."

"What now?" Mel asked, and could have sworn he saw the man kiss the cross that hung from his neck.

Somehow they got to shore and back to their miserable hotel. San Blas was supposed to be a hot hippie retreat, and Mel was hoping for a wild time of it. But the hotel was deserted except for a girl bartender who seemed to be doubling as a hooker. Tense from the day, Mel accepted the hook, excusing himself. "This is turning out to be some trip," said Lonnie, left to his own devices at the bar, drinking a Pacifica beer apparently contemplating his present and future relationship with Karen, while Mel himself play-acted the closest thing to love that life's theater seemed to offer him that night.

The next day, they were off to Guadalajara and spent their days exploring all the haunts Mel knew plus a few new ones, ending their evenings with fantastic tacos at El Farol and other spots, then sitting around listening to the mariachis competing in the Plaza Tapatía, and then over to the surrounding bars, where they saw comedians and heard songs they couldn't quite grasp, begged off the bargirls, and ended half-drunk listening to boleros about lost loves and who knew what else.

Finally, they took the night bus to Mexico City, breezing through Michoacán and arriving too early to look for a hotel. They dragged themselves over to a restaurant near the bus depot and were having their coffee, with Mel rattling on about this or that, when they could hear a marching band drawing near and then watched as people in the restaurant stood up from their seats.

"Stand up!" and older woman screeched at Lonnie in Spanish, and she even prodded him with the tip of her umbrella. "Don't you have any sense of respect?" she seemed to ask.

The two innocents abroad stood up, just as the band and dignitaries passed the restaurant door on their way to a little plaza near the bus station.

"This is President's Day," the waiter explained as the procession went by and people returned to their seats. "We're halfway through the presidency of Díaz Ordaz and there's lot of tension in the city, lots of young people protesting against the Olympics preparations and rising tuition at the UNAM."

"Maybe we should go to Acapulco now and come back when the tension's eased off," Lonnie said. "I don't feel like getting my head bashed in over some political stuff I don't even understand. Besides," he added, "I noticed they went after me and not you, and I think I'm learning something nasty about these Mexican friends of yours." That stated, they went back to the depot and booked themselves on the first bus they could find heading south.

Once there, they checked into the cheapest hotel Mel knew (he'd stayed there with his ex-wife some years before) and went for a late afternoon swim, cleaning up and going to the Quebrada for the nightly dive. The next day, they spent lolling at Caleta Beach and then jeeping it over to another beach to watch the sunset. That night, Mel was restless and couldn't be stopped as he hopped from bar to bar hoping to hook up and, failing, convincing Lonnie to take a taxi with him to the "Zona de Tolerancia," or red light district, where they found bar after bar of women dancing topless and sometimes bottomless with whoever. Heading to one of the least prosperous and cheapest-looking places, Mel provided Lonnie with the distinct pleasure and privilege of watching him choose one of the girls from a virtual lineup and take her into a backroom. Returning, he said it wasn't all that bad, that he'd been treated better than usual. Lonnie said nothing, but got them the cab to their hotel, where he immediately packed his things.

"What are you doing?" Mel asked, exhausted and ready to sleep.

"This can't go on," said Lonnie, "This is a bullshit trip, that isn't curing you of anything or helping you or me in any way. And it's time for me to start heading back."

111

Ashamed of his weakness, Mel also packed, and they cabbed it over to the bus depot in time to take the 6 a.m. bus back to Mexico City.

3.

Lonnie was set on leaving for San Diego as soon as possible, but I begged him to forgive me and suggested that we stay at least a few days, to visit the pyramids, the Zócalo, the Belles Artes, the university, the homes of Frida, Diego and Trotsky—you name it. I won out, and got him to agree to this plan which would round out the two weeks and give him time to see things he might never have a chance to see again. It all seemed to make perfect sense, especially since I had visited all these places and could make it easy for us both if I could just control my raging needs and complexes.

Off we went on our way, but at the very first venue examining the paintings at Belles Artes, we ran into Edith, a fine-looking woman from the U. of Wisconsin who had been travelling all over Mexico on her own. I showed off my great knowledge of Mexican art as I led her and Lonnie around. Then we went downstairs to buy tickets for the Ballet Folklórico that night and headed for the nearest cafe, where we talked of this and that and joked about everything, agreeing finally to hang out together in the city until it was time for her to take her plane back to Wisconsin.

That afternoon, after lunch, we cabbed over to the Anthropological Museum and went on a tour that filled us in about pre-Colombian Mexico. But I have to confess that the more we went around, the less I heard, and the more I grew infatuated with Edith, fantasying a great love affair in progress. The tour over, we lunched and then separated to rest awhile, agreeing to meet up at the Belles Artes performance. I said nothing to Lonnie about my growing feelings, but I guess they weren't too hard to figure out. All I know is that when we met in the lobby, I tried to work out the seating so that I sat between them, but Edith made a special point of changing things so that she sat between us, commenting to one and then the other about the production, inevitably leaning more in Lonnie's direction if only to avoid my persistent and transparent efforts to over-engage her. We agreed the show was great, charming and just maybe a little bit hokey, and then we wandered north up Avenida San Juan de Letrán making our way past the Teatro Blanquita to the Plaza Garibaldi where we listened to the mariachis, ending up at a bar restaurant where we ate tacos and drank beer as the night wore on. Finally we walked back down San Juan de Letrán and that's when I realized I was desperately jealous of the easy relationship my new love had with Lonnie. I tried to control it and didn't say a word as we cabbed it over to her hotel, with her kissing us both goodnight (though her kiss for Lonnie seemed longer and deeper), and leaving us to make it back home.

I was moody, hardly saying anything. Lonnie sensed something was wrong and asked what was going on.

"She likes you more than me," I said.

"Really!" Lonnie said with surprise, and then remained silent a second. "Well maybe she sees that I'm just friendly and that I've no ulterior motive," he added.

"And me?" I asked.

"You're like a wild animal stalking his prey," Lonnie said laughing. "You're leaning all over her."

Somehow our ambling walk to the hotel took us through one of the more fashionable streets of the fashionable Zona Rosa, where I held my breath as a sharp-looking woman dressed rather formally in black, and with black gloves, stopped us and asked where we from. We told her we were from San Diego, and she immediately suggested that she could go to our hotel room and give us both a beautiful evening. She was so attractive, all I could think of saying was "How much?"

113

She stated her price as "100 each."

"In dollars or pesos?" I asked.

"In dollars," she said, laughing gently.

"I'm afraid it's too much," I said. "Maybe we could have a special price?"

"No," she said, "it's the going market rate."

"Well, I wish we could, but it's just too much."

"Well, have a wonderful evening," she said, removing a glove to shake Lonnie's hand and then mine. "Have as good a night as you can without me."

"What was that about?" Lonnie asked. And I explained the encounter word for word. "Maybe we should've gone with her," he said, laughing at the encounter, "I notice she wasn't concerned about skin color and I don't think either one of us is going to have any luck with Edith—maybe me because I don't want to and you because you do!"

4.

The next morning they met Edith for breakfast at the Super Leche just down the street from the Torre Latina, and then the three explored the streets leading to the Zócalo and beyond, entering the Cathedral and touring Diego Rivera's murals in the Government building, and then gravitating toward a group of students gathered on a corner of the immense plaza, giving impassioned speeches which, Mel explained, dealt with Mexico's poverty, the plans to up university tuition, and all the money being spent to prepare for the summer Olympics. A big rally was planned for that night just after a special performance by the company of actor-director Alejandro Jodorowsky at a place called the Plaza of Three Cultures, otherwise known as or Tlatelolco. The threesome continued their touring, but made sure to arrive early at the Plaza in time for Jodorowsky's play. The place was famous for the imposition of a church and then a modern apartment complex over an important Aztec temple and the claim was that the Plaza represented all of Mexico and its history. This night, lots of people were milling about, but only some of them were going to the theater, and the friends were able to get tickets as well as the cellophane raincoats that for one reason or another were issued to all ticket buyers.

In the theater everyone seemed to jockey for the seats furthest from the stage, but the fearless threesome just latched on to a great set of seats in the third row. Suddenly the lights went down, some drums rolled, and psychedelic lights blinded and dazzled, as the curtain rose. Carnival music began and actors came running down both sides of the theater throwing candies and condoms at the audience and soon making their way on to the stage. Then some of the actors took off all their clothes, a few simulated lovemaking and maybe a few made love, while others pissed in pots placed around the stage and one actor seemed to defecate into a toilet that was somehow mounted on the head of another actor who was staring out at the audience in a state of bewildered meditation.

At this point the threesome heard large, amplified crowing sounds, and a mass of roosters, hens and chickens were released on to the stage, pursued by men and women naked except for their multi-colored Aztec waist skirts, their Aztec hair-plumes and the threatening daggers they flashed and thrashed as they chased the fowl around the stage. Soon they had captured some of the animals and proceeded to cut off their heads, throwing the headless bodies out into the audience. Blood splattered every which way, so that the raincoats and hoods helped but in no way fully protected anyone. Then the people kept screaming "*Más!*—More!" And then someone shouted "*Abajo con los corruptos,*" —"Down with the corrupt ones!" —while still others screeched, "*Abajo con Díaz Ordaz*"— "Down with Díaz Ordaz", "*Las olimpiadas a la mierda!*"—"Shit on the Olympic Games!"— and other charming chants.

Covered more with blood than almost anyone because of their absurd choice seats, the threesome followed the other spectators out of the theater and into the plaza area, where the crowd had gotten much larger and more inflamed, singing *The Internationale* and some Mexican Revolution corridos. Bull horns, seashells and party flutes filled the air; and then came repeats of the slogans they'd heard in the theater, plus "*Viva la Revolución!*" The threesome joined the crowd with great verve and delight singing the melodies even if they didn't know the words, hearing and cheering unintelligible speeches filled with menace and fire.

Word spread that the police were getting ready to move in if the rally persisted and that there would be a strategy meeting the next day to consider what could and should be done. It was going to be Edith's last day before her plane took off for home and they asked her if she wanted to do more tourism or keep apace with the developing crisis. She hesitated and then answered. "A little of both," she said laughing. "But really this political process is hotter and stickier than anything I've seen in Wisconsin."

"But why not stay longer?" they both asked, urging her to find a way to stay, but she said she was having boy-friend trouble and had to resolve what she was going to do.

"Stay with us," Lonnie said, "We'll help you decide."

"No," she said, laughing and giving Lonnie a kiss, "You guys are great, but I have to go back and deal with all this." Mel found himself turning morose. One thing was the boyfriend, but now he was convinced—it became ever more clear— that if Edith had doubts, it was because of Lonnie and not him.

When she went to the bathroom, Mel could not constrain himself. "It's so unfair," he said. "Here you have the steady girl and this one's falling for you too. And me, I'm the third wheel, the one who's being pushed aside."

116

"Don't look at it that way," Lonnie insisted. "She's thinking about her boyfriend while she's paling around with us. We're all torn between tourism and politics here, and none of it mixes with a Mexican love affair."

"No, you can't fool me," said Mel almost beside himself. "You and Edith have something going, and you just don't want to hurt my feelings by telling me." He was beside himself and then he went further than even he thought he'd be crazy enough to go. "You've got to promise me you're not going to bed with her," he said. "You've got to promise that even if I strike out, you won't try to get it on with her."

"Are you serious?" Lonnie asked, surprised and dismayed.

"Yes, I am," Mel answered, insistent even if ashamed.

"O.k.," said Lonnie pretending that it didn't matter any way because he was so fully committed to Karen. "But don't you feel kind of embarrassed to ask me to step aside, while it might be nicer and fairer to see who she really wanted if she wanted either of us."

"We both know who she'd go with, and I know it's really rotten of me, but I don't think I could stand it if she went with you— I think I'd go crazy and do something awful."

"In other words, you're blackmailing me," said Lonnie. "If I make love to Edith, I'm going to cause you to commit suicide or kill me."

"Think what you like," Mel said, "And I know it's not right, but that's what I need. And so I'm asking you to promise to not make love to her, and let me try to get somewhere with her."

"All right," Lonnie said looking at Mel in dismay. And Mel felt rotten about it, but he also knew he could not turn his back or recant; he knew he needed Lonnie's guarantee as a friend; and he knew that Edith would probably not be interested in him anyway; and he knew too that Lonnie's probably unnecessary guarantee would probably mark the beginning of the end of their close friendship.

5.

And so it was. We took her home and we both kissed her good night, and then called on her again early the next morning. Off we went sightseeing, having lunch together, and then making our way back to a meeting room on the grounds of the Plaza of Three Cultures. But when we tried to enter the meeting, we were asked for identification papers and our "affiliations"; and since we could provide no good answers, we were asked to leave. In fact, the situation turned downright hostile as we showed our U.S. documents, and some of the students called us *imperialistas*, *yanquis*, and spies, with things heating up until we decided it was time to leave.

Suddenly exiled from the exciting events playing out around us, reminded of our place in the Mexican order of things, cut adrift and running out of time, we made our way to the Zona Rosa, checking out the stores and each buying an Aztec trinket for Edith's beautiful charm bracelet. Edith also bought us gifts, luring us into a photo machine kiosk, taking pictures of the three and then one each with each of us, and then having the pictures put in frames that fit in our wallets. She wrote her name, address, and telephone number on each frame, each saying, "With love and for our never-to-forget Mexico City adventures, Edith."

All three of us were moved and we had a last margarita together. Then we took her off to her hotel, where a special van awaited to take her to the airport. We kissed her goodbye, and I took the opportunity to tell her, "I love you Edith, I want us to see each other again."

"Me too," she said, smiling and kissing me. "But let me see what I do about my boyfriend and let's see what you and Lonnie do."

We watched as Edith's van began on its way toward the airport, and then we went back to our hotel to get ready for our bus trip back to our hopefully waiting and repaired car.

"You know what?" said Lonnie, "Why don't we take a plane to Hermosillo and speed up the process?"

I agreed, so we paid our bill and took a cab to the airport, barely making the seven p.m. flight. We stayed the night in Hermosillo and then took the bus to Santa Ana, where my car awaited us, the mechanic turning out to be the honest Seven Day Adventist we'd hoped he would be.

Off we went, racing over to Sonoita, passing the checkpoint, and traveling along the border to Mexicali, where we then drove across. Lonnie insisted on driving so there're be no stops or detours or brothel appointments he was afraid I might arrange—and we'd get him home as soon as possible to his awaiting true love. Soon after passing Calexico, he stopped at a coffee shop and called Karen telling her he missed her and was racing home. She said she'd missed him too and loved him, and he told her he loved her too, almost crying with joy.

"Well, I guess it'll be time for me to move out of the house," I said, "as you guys settle in."

"You don't have to do that," Lonnie said, "Things can go on like before."

"You and I both know that won't work," I said. "I really thought I loved Edith," I added. "And I know only a true friend like you would agree not to hit on her when it was clear she was leaning more in your direction than in mine."

"But I told her about Karen," Lonnie answered.

"That's why she went back to see her boyfriend," I said.

"Well, maybe," Lonnie mused.

"Maybe like hell—it was clear as could be. And even though you're totally committed to Karen, I know it wasn't easy for you to withdraw just because I asked you to, and it was totally rotten of me to ask you to do it," I found myself repeating. "And then too, I keep thinking if I was so convinced Edith preferred you at least partly because you're black."

So there's some 'black male' in your blackmail," he said with a gentle laugh.

"Yes, and maybe that's another reason why I have to move out," I said, "even though I know now that I'll probably never call her and never want to see her and even damaged my friendship with you for a woman I'll probably never see, and probably wasn't ever really in love with in the first place."

"Still," I added as we headed past Lemon Grove on our way into San Diego, "it was a great trip to Mexico. And I learned more about Mexican politics than I ever knew before or ever really wanted to know, even though I didn't understand or really learn anything worth a damn. I guess we'll find out where all that anger led to later this summer. But no matter what, I also learned about you, me and us, and I'll always thank you for going with me, Lonnie, for the rest of my life."

México Profundo

"South of the Border Down Mexico Way"

1.

Mel traveled along the Mexican side of the border once again, but this time in his near new station wagon before turning south past Mazatlán and on to Guadalajara where he would take his first formal classes in Spanish and live for six weeks in a Mexican city. His days on the road were uneventful enough, as he slept in the back of the wagon and cruised from town to town and bar to bar.

The first few days in Guadalajara he stayed with a middle-class Mexican family, but he all but gagged on an arrangement that was too restrictive for a man of his age and needs. He dreaded the dinner conversations about *Readers Digest* condensed books and trips to Sears in Houston. He broke his residential contract and moved into a small apartment complex in a working-class district of the city and began to live a more Mexican life as soon as he got off from his classes at school.

The classes were fine, even with a teacher whose main technique was to throw a ball at a student who had to respond properly to her phrase in Spanish. Then there was the toxic professor who wasted his students' time by his longwinded anecdotes which were mainly to assert that his summer gringo students came from a racist culture while he and other Mexican *dons* knew how to take care of their *indios*, treating them quite well, gracias, unless they forgot their place.

That was the morning, but what to do with the long afternoons and evenings, even if one spent some time studying? Mel soon realized that almost all the American women were dating young Mexicans and learning all the ins and outs of the city and beyond, while the respectable *mexicanas* were mainly off limits to the gringo men, who spent most of their time getting drunk, dancing and bedding "bar girls." Mel had nothing against the girls and in fact enjoyed his encounters with them for all he learned far beyond the mere joy of sex. But the days were passing, and passing his precious time that way just wasn't compelling or agreeable enough for him. At first, he explored the possibilities in his new environment, feeling drawn to one maid working there, Lupe; but she didn't seem to respond to his hints and more overt advances, and soon he resigned himself to thinking nothing would happen on that front.

2.

Mel's assessment might have proven correct had he not embarked on an endeavor that went out from the apartment complex in which he lived and out beyond what he thought were his moral boundaries. One day, reading the newspaper, he realized that many visiting men put adds in the paper seeking girls willing to serve as "maids." Imitating the Spanish of the ads he studied, Mel wrote his own none too ambiguous message, asking for "someone to clean his house and converse with him in Spanish, etc." delivered it to the paper, paid his fee and waited to see if there were any results.

Mel knew that what he was doing was wrong; it shamed him above all because it went against the grain of his growing awareness of things. But he could not repress or control his desires or his outright curiosity and excitement about this experiment. There was something the seemed liberating in doing things of which he did not approve.

Sure enough, a woman came to his door, and then came another. He invited the first one in, interviewed her, sizing her up, and was disappointed when on telling her that his real interest was for a summer sex partner, she blushed and, laughing, said no thanks, she had a boyfriend and was just looking for work. Another girl knocked on the door one morning, and when she heard his rap, said she couldn't do that, but if he wanted to pay her enough for a quickie that would cover her loss of time and bus fare, she would oblige him. He would have easily paid her more for her trouble, but he couldn't resist accepting her offer, ending up in the shower with her and then making pleasant love with her in his bed. Getting up, she gave him her telephone number and said he could call her if he wanted to date her, and she left.

By this time, several of the tenants and of course all the maids who cleaned rooms and changed bedding in the complex where he lived had read his add and knew why at least a few women were coming to the apartment looking for him. He, in fact, knew that some of the maids provided sexual services for the men in the building, but they seemed to be quite reluctant to take him on, perhaps because he was a gringo just there for a short stay or because their current clients might object. However, after his second encounter, one of the girls, María, came into his room and said she was tired of having to deal with the women who came looking for him. She clearly wanted some compensation.

Mel found her homely and very sexy. He felt his desire growing and said, "why don't you come in, María so that we can talk?" She understood what he wanted immediately, and said she couldn't right now but would come back soon. That morning, Mel cut his classes for the first time as he waited for María. But when she came to see him, his excitement was at its limits. He entered her and climaxed almost immediately.

"*Cochino*," she cried out, laughing and getting up, clearly waiting for some recompense. Mel reached for his wallet and handed her the few pesos he had on him. "*¿Eso es todo?*" she shrieked.

"That's all I have today," he said, "but I can get more . . . "

"*Eres el más codo que he visto*—you're the cheapest guy I've ever been with," she said, "Next time you need me, don't bother asking."

123

"But María—" he said, hoping to renegotiate the arrangement and looking forward to further encounters, but she went off in a huff.

Maybe he could have righted things with María with a second gift, but other girls came to visit, and even audition, and then an older woman almost in her fifties came to him and said María had sent her.

"Well, why would she do that when she said I was a cheap bastard, not worth her time?" he asked.

"Oh, she just said that because the old man she services wasn't going to let her make it with another man in the complex."

"Oh," said Mel, thinking he understood now.

"Anyway, she knew I needed work and said you might like me. So I thought maybe I could make love to you and you could think about it." Mel was hardly attracted to this woman, but she seemed nice enough, and she certainly knew how to prepare a man, so before you knew it, he made love to her, paid her quite generously and told her he'd call if he wanted to see her again or make something more of it.

Two days later his penis had swollen, and it was obvious to him that this woman had given him his first case of the clap. Maybe that was the real reason why María sent her to him, he mused; but he went to the school infirmary, got the penicillin treatment and was told to lay off sex for two weeks. He passed a night in fever, and the next morning, he found Lupe, the shyest girl of the complex staff, wiping the sweat from his brow.

"What happened?" he asked.

"You were very sick and delirious, some of the tenants heard you screaming and said I should see you." And there she was, and he was thankful and happy she was with him.

"You shouldn't be seeing all those women," she said, laughing, "especially if María sent them. And if you wanted to be with a nice girl, why didn't you just ask me?"

"Because I never thought you'd say yes," he explained. "You're so shy, and you just wouldn't flirt with me or anything."

"I don't usually mess around," she said, "I just do my job and make the best I can of things."

"Would you like to be my summer girl?" he said. "I can pay you ok, and we can be friends too. You can teach me Spanish, and we can go out to some places too."

"Well," she said, "I know you're going to pay someone anyway, so why not me?" she laughed. "Besides I might even like the sex," she said laughing again.

The truth of the matter was that while Mel had considered Lupe, clearly, if he'd wanted to take up with her, he'd have asked. Somehow, he had sensed something in her that was perhaps too sad or too deep. He was afraid of the complications. But he had to admit he felt some strong sense of tenderness if not passion for her and was now eager to test the waters.

Of course, there was nothing he could do that day or the next few, but she did come back after her chores and stayed in bed with him, nursing him and kissing him and making him feel pretty damned good. When he recovered, he went out, had a pharmacist check him and asked how long he should wait before he resumed any sexual activity.

"Well, you should wait a few weeks."

"That's too long!" he complained.

"Well, it won't hurt you to start as soon as you get the urge—and as for the girl, just give her the courtesy of using a sombrero."

125

He bought a pack of rubbers, and the next day, when Lupe came to see him, they officially began what would be their month-long plus summer romance.

3.

It was certainly a rather limited affair and a rather melancholy one at that. First of all, he found that Lupe had a boy and that she had to be home by late afternoon, which meant he could never take her out at night and suffered the same evening solitude he'd experienced before he'd bedded her. But worst of all, while he found her to be the sweetest of women, he soon learned, as he had feared, that she knew virtually nothing about giving and receiving pleasure. He might achieve orgasm, but she'd just lie there passively. So, while she helped his Spanish by speaking that language and only that language all the time they were together, he spent all his time trying to teach her how to free herself from a repression that ran so deep. In fact, while she never refused him and seemed to enjoy their extended times in bed together, he felt a great sadness at failing to open her up to sexual desire and passion. And that made it hard for him to stay hard and at least derive some minimal pleasure from their encounters.

"Lupe," he once told her, "you're making me feel like a real flop in bed."

And she answered, no she loved her time with him and besides her doctor said it was doing her good. She was less nervous and irritable, had less pain in her back and legs. It was good to know he was having a therapeutic effect; but even though they both knew this was a typical gringo-tapatía summer affair, he wanted to have at least the illusion that his time with her would help them both for the rest of their lives.

Their usual routine was for him to come home from classes and wait for her to get off from work in the early afternoon. Then they would spend some time in his room or go to the park or an early movie, and then he would drive her to home in Zapópan, at that time a small suburb just outside the city proper. Increasingly, and perhaps because of their limited sex life, he would take her for a drive out to Lake Chapala or some other area. There they would try the local cuisine and rent a room for an hour or two of intimacy before he dropped her off near her house and then head back to town for a night or weekend on his own. Some of these days were pleasant enough, as they explored places they had never been before. And during their rides and time together, bits and pieces of her life came more and more to his attention.

She was born and raised in a *rancho* outside of the town of Pénjamo, a place made famous by a song which told about some *campesinos* getting back to what was a speck on the map but was for them the biggest center in their region and their world. Clearly, an uncle had abused her at an early age. Her first boyfriend had beaten and raped her, leaving her pregnant and labeled a whore by her neighbors and her own parents. With virtually no education, she'd come to Guadalajara and had met María who'd gotten her a job and, it turned out, eventually urged her to take up with him.

With his nights and weekends all too free, Mel came to know a variety of women, including some visiting *americanas* as the summer rolled on. But he added no new lovers, and he spent most of his time thinking of Lupe, piecing together her story, so typical, he realized, of so many he'd heard about the youth of countless poor Mexican girls. Mel could fully understand her difficulties with sexual pleasure, the repression of pleasure, the effects of being *indígena-mexicana*, of being poor and female from the most humble rural background, from being still after centuries a subservient colonial subject. Perhaps it was pity, but a feeling of tenderness pervaded him in his feelings for her, especially as the days passed into weeks, and his time with her was already coming to a close.

4.

One thing he wanted to do before he returned to California was to take the smallest trip with her. He thought of Puerto Vallarta or Manzanillo or even Barra de Navidad. But she decided on the place, telling him one day that she had some days free and she wanted him to take her to her hometown. Mel got his station wagon ready, and off they went traveling east out toward Michoacán, passing through the center of some of the towns along the way, as they took a circuitous route toward Pénjamo. When they got to La Piedad, something went wrong with the wheel rigging, but the local mechanic twisted some hangers and set them in place, saying this should hold for about five-hundred miles—certainly long enough to get them to get to Pénjamo and back. "That's how we are," Lupe told him. "We do what we can with what comes our way."

Soon enough they were indeed arriving in the famously miserable town, passing *rancho* after *rancho*, until she excitedly directed him to make a left and then a right, and they found themselves on the site of her early abuse, but also the greatest love she had experienced in her life.

"There it is!" she exclaimed, pointing to a small group of structures, one of which must have been the house and another a manger, given the small group of cows and pigs lolling about the property. But Lupe made no move to step down from the car.

"Let's go to the center of town and get you a place to stay," she said. Soon they checked into a hotel and checked out the bed, making love in the afternoon as was their custom, with her seeming to be enjoying it, so happy she was to be home after so long.

"Listen," she said, "you'll have to stay here while I visit my father," she said. "Then you can come by in the morning and see the place and meet my family."

Mel had somehow imagined a scenario like this and had brought things to read—and then, of course, there was a TV. But he took her back near the *rancho* so she'd only have the shortest walk to get to where she was going.

He dropped her off, with her kissing him on the cheek, and him watching as she made her way toward her house. He drove back to his hotel, happy to find that the place had a small swimming pool and he spent the afternoon doing laps, reading and taking a few drinks from the bar. Night came on, and he strolled through the town, even entering a *cantina* to savor the local ambiance. Then he went up to the room and watched a Mexican movie on TV, wondering how Lupe was doing and then going off to sleep.

The next morning when he awoke, she was sitting at his bedside in tears.

"What happened?" he asked. But she seemed unable to speak. "Let's have some breakfast," he said.

He got up and dressed, and they went down to the breakfast room, her just picking at some eggs and coffee while telling him what had happened at the *rancho*.

"At first, they were so happy to see me but disappointed because I didn't bring my boy, and then they got mad thinking about how I'd dishonored them. When I told them that I came with an American friend, my father told me I shouldn't bring you over, and he got mad and called me a whore all over again after all these years. So, I told them to go to hell, and that I'd never come back. And then I went and hitched a ride, and here I am."

He checked out of the hotel, and they started back toward Guadalajara, taking side roads that took them past lakes and artisan villages. They went out on a large lake and ate a wonderful grilled fish. Then they headed back into town, and he dropped her off at Zapópan.

129

"I'm sorry," he said feebly, kissing her on her moist eyes.

"Don't worry," she said, "that's how things are here."

5.

The summer had worn on, and now he had just some days before he had to leave. He became concerned about how he would say goodbye and how they would each handle it all. He took her to a few stores and had her pick out two beautiful dresses; then, carefully skirting the rings, he bought her a lovely necklace with matching earrings that dangled and framed her face. Passing a music store, he bought her a few albums with songs they both had liked. She cried over the gifts but especially the dresses.

"You're just dressing me up for another lover," she blurted out.

"It isn't that, Lupe, I just want you to be pretty as can be," he managed to say—but then he could not resist adding "and yes, to have a happy life."

Just two days before his departure, she told him she would have to leave early and asked if he could María give a lift. There she was—his crazy go-between, an inspiration for some of his evening masturbations, as homely and sexy as ever, now mounting the station wagon, laughing, and sharing secrets with his summer love. Why were they so happy and squirmy when he was agonizing over his upcoming farewell? And when he looked at them in the rearview mirror, he realized that Lupe was wearing one of the dresses he'd bought and, lo and behold, María was wearing the other. And when he looked even closer, he realized that each of them was wearing one of the earrings he'd given her, and they were both laughing as freely as he had ever seen either one of them laugh.

He said nothing about what he saw, drove out toward the church which housed Zapópan's famous virgin when Lupe suddenly told him to take one side street and then another until they found a secluded spot.

"*Mira, mi amor*, you've bought me so many nice things, and I have nothing to give you except one special memory from your trip. Because I know you wanted to be with María again and to tell you the truth she's been crazy to be with you all summer, so now, we can all three be together."

And with that, the girls helped Mel fold down his back seat of his station wagon to make a bed with his mattress. With night setting in and no fear of interruption, they shared a bottle of tequila that María had brought for the occasion. They kissed and hugged and giggled and drank until desire hit them and Mel found himself entering María while he gave Lupe the best tonguing of the many he'd tried during the summer. Things came to a boil, and all three came in a rush. María called out "¡ya ya ya!" And Lupe seemed almost to sing as she came fully, wonderfully—perhaps, he figured, for the first time in her life. Then they kissed and drank and played some more until he was ready once again and, switching positions, they culminated the passions that had been building over the summer weeks.

The next day, Mel had much business to do, and the following day, he met with Lupe once again, this time all tenderness and sweetness, making love to her and, in fact, making her come again, but now without a chorus or accompaniment. Then he took her to the city's most wonderful antojitos place, where, as they shared some treats and a final *flan*, he took out a small but lovely ring and gave it to her saying he would never forget her and would try to see her in December when school went on break. She said she couldn't write him, but he should write her, and she'd get someone to read the letter and help her answer, and he said he would write but not be able to say all the things he might wish to. She said she

131

understood, but Mel sensed she knew this back and forth might never really occur. Then it was time for her to go, and he took her home, kissing her as he dropped her off, as he had done on so many summer days, only this time they knew it was the last.

6.

The next morning, he packed his station wagon and drove out of the city, making it to Nayarit and turning down toward San Blas and the nearest beach hotel. That night, the manager offered him a woman, but he said he was too depressed and turned in. Swimming in the early morning, he then paid his bill and started the steep climb out of San Blas to the main highway north. Then the wheel held by clothes hangers began to give out; and his wagon, forced to labor up the hill, finally reached the point of no return, as the radiator heated up and with a dying gasp blew its gasket and the motor with it. Sometime later he hitched his way to Tepíc, got a tow for the car and, virtually without cash, made an illegal sale of the wagon for enough money to get him to the border and maybe beyond. Later in the afternoon, he was on a bus to Mazatlán, where he checked in at the Hotel del Cima and went swimming on the beach in the morning. When he came out, he found his shoes had been stolen, and he had to buy some *chancla*s in the hotel boutique and walk into town to buy a new pair of shoes.

Coming back to the hotel, he took a swim in the pool and met a woman from Arizona, a schoolteacher who'd come down for a week away from the desert. Flirting away, he convinced her to go to dinner with him. He then withdrew to his room and took a nap, asking to be called at 6:45 p.m. Then he awoke and went so far as to call the woman to confirm their date. But when he reached her room and even raised his arm to knock on the door, he found himself lowering it and retreating down the hall. Part of it was the money— he was too low on funds to start something new; but part of it was Lupe, who hovered over his mind and made this casual adventure all too superficial to be worth pursuing.

Early the next morning, he checked out of the hotel and boarded a bus for Nogales, crossing there, and then taking the extra ride to Tucson, calling his father to tell him he'd be arriving on Greyhound the next day. In the evening, he walked the Tucson streets and saw how the Spanish had imposed their grid by cutting straight lines over the original indigenous spaces and demarcations. Then he noticed how all the downtown streets were labeled numerically one way and alphabetically the other. This had to be the Anglo contribution to Indian and Mexican life. And he imagined how bulldozers swept across the space, pushing Indians, Mexicans, and even some Blacks this way and that, crushing and grinding up those who couldn't get out of the way. This was how they did it, and maybe how he had followed their lead in Guadalajara, it occurred to him now.

Just hours later, he was on the bus to Los Angeles; and after a few days with his parents, he would make his way back to San Diego.

Lolita, Almost

1.

For sure Mel was never going to take up with such a girl. She was Jewish from Amsterdam but no Anne Frank. Nor was she Hans Brinker's sister, nor the postcard young Dutch girl—both named Gretel, with the name apparently borrowed from the Grimm Brothers tale—she seemingly so pristine with her hair in braids. But her story did have its grim and grimy sides; and there was something frozen, but more like stone than ice, since her name was Petra—closer to the story perhaps of one or more of the hookers in the city's raucous red-light district, the story, he believes to this day, of an abused half-Jewish blonde girl—Jewish or not so Jewish after all—on her father's side who for years was Daddy's sweetie and who tried as hard as she could to fend against the abuse, but in the end, accepted it as her lot, finding it easier to please daddy and keep their little doings a secret—especially since her mother lived in total denial of what she must have known.

Petra had learned how to please men, learned what they liked and lusted for, what they wanted and how they wanted it. She could get her way with them, manipulate them, and enjoy the play, enjoy too her own little sweet orgasms, while feeling little or nothing for those who helped her get them.

She was some eight years his junior, had been his student, her skinny face and long neck at first drawing him away only to later draw him in, especially given her longish nose and roundish cheeks. He had been impressed over all by her writing, her ability to analyze coldly, ironically, always reducing human motives to petty instincts, always showing men for the ridiculously infantile and needful creatures they were, only successful because of their physical power and their sense of privilege, but in the last analysis ready to do anything to get what they so needed or wanted of women. She had it all down, had memorized the book, and each piece she wrote for his class simply played out different dimensions and variations of the cynical chess game she or life as we knew it had devised.

It was only after the course ended and she had her A, that she started insinuating herself into Mel's life. She sat in on his next class, where he moved from existential to social themes, probing the contemporary world, reading Marx, Mao, Frantz Fanon, Malcolm X and Eldridge Cleaver, Luis Valdez and Alurista, followed by Paul Goodman, Norman O. Brown, Herbert Marcuse, and even some early feminist texts as academia went through its transformations. The room was alive with revolution, sex and resistance against the war. The students and professor went to anti-war and civil rights rallies. The students lived out and wrote about their aberrant sexual inclinations—they summarized their experiences in class, while the professor was almost paralyzed by all he heard; and then came the little insinuations which Petra would make with her eyes and lips, or by sticking her finger penis-like in her mouth while crossing her eyes in some semblance of sexual obsession.

"Can we talk about the class some time?"

"Yes," he said, "why don't you meet me in my office..."

"Can't we meet off campus so we can really talk?"

He didn't feel at all attracted to her—his own interest in Latin women had become almost compulsive; but perhaps that made it easier for him to meet with her, because he believed himself to be immune to any provocations that she might try to send his way. So finally, he agreed to meet her in a brightly lit kosher-style deli not too far from campus. It was there that she proceeded to confess to him her affair with Daddy.

"How do you feel about all this?" he asked, shamed at the conduct of a fellow Jew, shocked too, as if despite his own anti-Semitism, this was beyond what he naively imagined any Jew to be capable of. "Do you still see him?"

"No," she said, "but he sometimes sends me money."

"And your mother?"

"She knew but never did anything even when I just about told her all of it. But she was afraid. He was a holocaust survivor and could get violent. She let his past be his excuse with me. I guess she kind of gave up on helping me and focused on my brother. She lives here but I hardly see her."

In his own mind he'd figured out her motivation. She was a lonely child rejected by a father who'd done her terrible wrong and now didn't want to be constantly reminded by seeing her but sent her money to allay his guilt feelings. Her mother had also rejected her, so she was like an orphan seeking a parent, and that parent was the nice and not abusive older Jewish male—him, Mel.

He couldn't help but feel compassion for her as she told her story, but in the middle of it, she came over to his side of the booth they were sharing, and put her head on his shoulder.

And at that moment he grew tense. "Look Petra," he started. "You're a wonderful, pretty girl and I have the deepest feelings for what you've been through, but you're way too young and I can't play daddy, because I'm already going with a very nice woman who's right for my age and situation."

With this, she suddenly looked up at him with her deep blue eyes, and said, "But honey, I know you don't have another girlfriend, and I was just going to try to help you."

"Help me?" he said, taken aback. "But why would I need help?"

136

"All the girls in the class know you need help—we talk about it all the time. All your talk about being and nothingness, politics and revolution, race and sex and all—and we all know you don't have a girlfriend, and we all know the women you tried to get with and failed."

"Look," he said, "even if what you said were true, that wouldn't make me want to take up with you. A girl who's been hurt like you is liable to be harboring desires for revenge, and I might be setting myself up for real trouble."

"Well, everything's a risk, you know," she said, "But I think we'd really be good for each other, if only for a time. We might even have fun too."

"Look," he told her, "You're young and lovely, you have a right to your youth and all the happiness you can find. But it's just not going to be with me."

And with that he steered her to his car, and started driving her back to the dorms where she was living, apparently on daddy's guilt money. But as they reached the complex on campus, she went right for his fly, rubbing oh so gently. "You know you don't mean this. You know you've got a good-looking girl in your car who'd love to spend the night with you, so why don't you stop playing Mr. Mature Professor and let me kiss away all your pain."

And suddenly he couldn't resist. She kept touching and kissing him, licking his face like a Cheshire cat in heat. She massaged his tense neck muscles, she intruded her tongue between his lips; and before he knew it he was embracing her with passion, thinking maybe he could help her and now desperately wanting to hold her as tightly as he could.

They ended up at his apartment and the lovemaking was beautiful and exciting. She sighed and orgasmed so sweetly and with such gentle pleasure, that he found himself probing her as deeply as he could, knowing that it was all mistake, it would all turn out badly, but now unable to help himself at all.

2.

When he awoke the next morning, he found her wearing his bathrobe and her hair up under a towel. Clearly, she'd showered and cleaned and was now actually making some breakfast even as she sought to straighten out his kitchen chaos.

"You really need a woman's touch, sweetie."

"Now don't start taking over my life," he said. "Last night was great but today we have to get back to reality."

"But this is reality, honey. We're here, it's Saturday morning, and we've nothing to do but clean up the kitchen, have some breakfast and make love all afternoon." It was hard to resist such an agenda, but he was as wary as he could be, given his circumstances and weakness.

"Fine, fine," he said, "but don't start getting any ideas about moving in here—that's just pushing things too far."

"I wasn't even thinking about such a thing!" she explained, "But thanks for offering."

"That wasn't an offer—it was a no in anticipation."

"Whatever you say sweetie," and she turned to continue her kitchen work. He looked at her a moment, and felt the urge to hug her from behind, rub against her surprisingly broad-beamed rear, and then make love to her as he had done the night before. But he resisted until they breakfasted on the eggs, potatoes, coffee, and juice that she'd prepared just right. At which point, he tried to kiss her, and she brushed him aside. "Go take a shower," she told him. "Don't be such a dirty old man."

He accepted this reproof like a little boy and went off to shower and shave and get ready for mommy, or daughter or whoever she was or wanted to be.

When he came out of the bathroom, he caught her in the last stages of moving his TV into the bedroom and then setting it up so they could watch things together from his bed.

"See?" he said. "Now you're trying to change my world," he protested.

"I already have, sweetheart," she told him. "But you just let me know if you want me to stop." He knew she had him at least for now, and within a few minutes they were in bed watching some stupid programs when, before he could think twice, they were caressing and kissing until one thing just led to another.

Sitting up some time later, he asked her to tell him more about her life, about how she faced her high school teachers and fellow students carrying the secret about her father. Did she have normal dates, crushes, back-of-car explorations?

"Of course, I did honey, I liked to make love with everybody. I mean, if you've made love to your old man, why not make love to everyone?"

"Boys as well as men?"

"Yes."

"Girls as well as boys?"

"Of course!" she told him sweetly without batting an eye and giving him a kiss as well.

"Have you ever been with two women?" she asked.

"No," he lied, "have you?"

"Well, almost," she said, "but the boyfriend of one of the girls came home so we just did what we could…"

"You mean a ménage à quatre?"

"Is that what they call it?" she asked, though she seemed more the teacher than the student on this turf.

"It's just that I can get turned on by almost anything at any time; and I learned very young that the only limits were the ones we chose to impose. So, I learned to give in to everything and enjoy everything."

"So have you been in orgies?" he asked.

"Well not the usual kind, I guess. But last summer, I was with some friends camping and I got up early and went down to the river where I found a group of guys swimming naked. Before I knew it, they spotted me and waved and shouted that I should join them. And I just couldn't resist, I just took off my clothes and jumped in the water, and swam and played with them, doing all kinds of crazy things. I had one penis in my hand and another in my mouth and one in my cunt and one in my ass. And we all had such a good time sucking and coming…"

He couldn't believe what he was hearing, and he wondered if it were true, but at the same time his erection had been growing as he heard the story, and she was very much aware of it. "I had one penis in one hand," she repeated, touching and teasing him as he grew hard in her hand, "and I had my clit grinding on this other guy's face," she added, varying her story as she sucked on his balls and staff, while gyrating her clitoris against his hungry tongue, until they both reached the next climax of their afternoon in bed.

When evening came, they both agreed to leave the apartment and take a walk in the port, stopping for a drink and looking at the stars. It was she who broke the mood and curtailed his plans for a night like the last.

"I have to go home and clean up, honey. My mom's coming over for breakfast tomorrow morning," she explained. "Let's not see each other until Wednesday," she suggested, "so we can think about where we're at and where we might want to go."

It was all so reasonable and correct, and yet he found himself missing her already—this rather special young girl who seemed to be getting under his skin even as he found danger in all she said and at least claimed to do.

3.

Deny her as he tried, all the time knowing this could not ever be the love of his life, still he awaited Wednesday to see how this story would go. It's true that part of him wondered if her story about her mother coming to visit was true or if she'd had a prior date with one of her lovers. He knew it shouldn't matter, but it irked him to have no sense of who this girl really was and where he really stood. She did indeed call him on Wednesday morning, asking how he was and where they might go that evening. He paused and she told him about a movie she wanted to see. "We can go there, and I promise to be a good girl," she said, "especially if you buy me some popcorn."

It was Daddy's little girl, he felt, but he couldn't help but enjoy holding her hand and kissing her lightly, watching the movie at least with one eye, while keeping his other on her. True to her word, she made no advances except to accept the kiss and his warming hand. The picture over, they got in the car, and he wasn't sure if he should take her to her place or his. "Why don't you drop me off?" she said. "Too much to do tomorrow but promise to keep the weekend free for us."

And so, they met again on Friday evening, and he drove her across the border and down the toll road to Ensenada, where they stayed the night in his favorite French motel and then crossed the street for a French breakfast in the town's only French restaurant.

They drove out of town to Estero beach, where they walked awhile and had a late morning cocktail. They went to the Bufadora blow hole and hid among the rocks, with him kissing her and then actually going down on her, kissing and tonguing her until she gave out the loveliest of sighs, just as the sea-spray spread over the rocks and rained down upon them.

On Sunday, they drove back home early and went to his apartment. She seemed so happy. "It's so nice, sweetie, being with you. I think I should move in soon so we can love each other day and night."

"Don't even think about it," he chided.

"We could save some money too, and use it all for a beautiful trip."

"Go to sleep," he said, feeling his rising passion beginning to ebb with the talk.

"But make love to me first, sweetie," she said, and he did, but this time he did so out of some senseless sense of duty.

4.

She didn't move in, but became his weekend regular, and even kept her own sets of clothing for bed and going out, her own toiletries and sundries, so she didn't have to cart things back and forth. Mel convinced himself that this was a temporary situation. He was sticking with his Latina love project, but this lovely, sexy, maybe crazy girl was certainly a sweet if sometimes threatening adventure in the meantime. It is true that the danger signs appeared often enough. One female friend informed him Petra had been bragging to everyone about how she had the hotshot professor on her string.

'They're all alike," she was purported to say. "Once you get them to go to bed with you, they want you all the time. They think your vagina belongs to them and that's when you can really play

142

with their minds until they don't know what's up or down." He couldn't believe she was so calculating behind her sweet and innocent face. But on the other hand, how could one doubt the capacity of manipulation this young woman had?

It seemed to him they were both free, and he certainly dated other women, mainly Latinas, from time to time. But none of them entered his life with such intimacy, with her somehow forcing him to tell her of all his sexual adventures including all the mishaps, kissing away his disappointments, and urging him to enjoy one orgasm after another. Above all he told her of his Jewish adventures in high school and beyond—his juvenile love for Susan and how she'd grounded him up like a stone; his lost love for Ellen, for Maxine Lambrini, for Sylvia and Laura Rachel, until he'd had it with the Jewish women and found his way toward his Italian American wife and all the suffering she'd entailed. It was all getting too thick with growing intimacy, with growing chance for hurt. It was getting all too serious and without any easy way out.

Sure enough, to make matters worse, he received a call from his niece Irene saying that things were going very badly at home, and she wanted to come down for the weekend. He broke the news to Petra, and she seemed quite upset.

"Here we are, weekend lovers and now you're going to let this woman break into our space."

"That woman's my niece," he answered. "I love her and I have to try and help her out."

"And what am I supposed to do, sit at home, trimming my nails like some two-bit whore?"

"Come over," he said at last. "Come over on Saturday and hang out with us, go with us wherever we go."

"You mean that, sweetie? You promise not to be ashamed of me or lock me in the closet?"

143

"No," he said emphatically, though he was really holding his breath thinking of the complications that might pop up. "Be with us as much as you want."

5.

Soon enough, Irene arrived for her first and only visit with her uncle. He took her to the Kosher-style deli, and she told him of all her troubles and confusions. She hated being in a community college, she hated living at home, hated her mother, her sister, her life. He urged her to consider moving out, to come to San Diego. He could perhaps house her if her parents would pay the tuition. He could maybe get her a job—smooth the way. She wasn't convinced but she was listening, as they drove to his apartment and prepared themselves for bed. But just at that moment Petra called and asked if she could come over.

"Sure," he said, with some trepidation, which he tried to hide. "Just give me awhile to settle Irene in."

With that, he sat down with Irene and told her the situation. "Listen, Irene, I'm involved with a young woman just about your age. I hope you won't be upset, but she says she's really lonely, and wants to sleep over. Besides, she says she really wants to meet you and wants to see if we can pal around over the weekend."

What could Irene do but assent to the situation? "No problem," she said. "I've never met one of your girlfriends since the divorce."

"Believe me, most of them weren't worth knowing."

"But this one is?"

"Well, she's a different person, she's different from all the girls I've dated. But she's way too young for me. She's had a lot of trouble in her life, and I'm afraid this isn't going to work out. But for now, I'm kind of in the thick of things."

"Are you in love with her?" she asked.

And he found himself confounded. "No," he said, "not at all. … Well, maybe a little, because I sympathize so much with her, and I spend a lot of time trying to make her happy—it's hard to explain."

Before he could go any further, Petra arrived, a small suitcase in hand and clearly set to pass the whole weekend with them. "Hello," she said, giving him a kiss and then greeting Irene, the two young girls, eyeing each other, Irene clearly taken aback, to see that this girl roughly her own age was having an affair with her only uncle whom she knew to be a bit unorthodox to say the least. A few beers went around, and the girls made some jokes about the kinds of men available on the dating scene.

Then came the time to go to bed. And he said, "Irene, I hope it doesn't bother you, but I guess Petra and I will be sleeping together."

"No," she said, she didn't mind. But it seemed to him that she did.

To make matters worse, Petra insisted in making love to him, working on him until he could resist no more, making more noise than she ever did before. "You bitch!" he whispered as she came in an exaggerated way, and she laughed louder than he had ever heard her.

6.

The next morning, he awoke to the clang of pots as the two girls were making breakfast in the kitchen. He pretended to be asleep so he might get some sense of their interaction even though he couldn't make out their words. He could hear Irene speaking in low tones and apparently commenting like a church choir while Petra, so often as quiet as a bottle, was suddenly the leader of the congregation, enunciating the key phrases to which his niece responded. It all sounded like girlie talk—about hair, diaphragms, and weird experiences with odd and old men pretty much like him.

145

With a sigh of relief, he pretended to wake up and suddenly kissed them both good morning and commented that his two favorite young ladies seemed to be getting along fine; and with them assenting with giggles and looks at each other, he sat down for coffee, and asked them what they wished to do for the day. Neither seemed to have a plan, so he suggested a day at Balboa Park or the beach. "The beach!" they both agreed. And so it was.

He drove them over to Point Loma past the immense cemetery to the lighthouse looking over the San Diego area and down beyond the border. Then he took them to Shelter Island, past Sea World and out toward Mission Bay and Mission Beach. There he parked and they went on to the sand, the steel-blue water still too cold for swimming, but the sandy expanse just fine for walking. This they did for a while and then sat and talked about Irene's life and problems, with him trying to get Petra to help him convince her that she needed to get away from her family and that maybe San Diego could be a solution for her. After a while the clouds came in and it started to darken, so they left the beach and headed for lunch. "Well, it looks like we go to Balboa, or we cross the border," he said.

Irene stopped eating, clearly unnerved—to cross the border with this uncle was perhaps too much to contemplate. But Petra was enthusiastic. "Yes, let's go!" she said. "We'll get him to spend some of his professor money buying us something and then we'll eat out and we'll have a fine time!"

The enthusiasm was contagious, and Irene agreed to go. "But don't take me to any of those dirty bars, no horses mounting women—none of that."

"Of course not," Petra said, "though it might be fun to see."

"Agh," he said. And Irene just fumed and sputtered.

Then, off they went down the road. A half an hour later, they were walking from block to block on Avenida Revolución, going from store to store, putting up with the hawkers with their sales pitches and insinuations, until they finally found a special place selling all kinds of wrought iron earrings in the most original designs. Both girls were fascinated by what they saw. But Irene resisted. They're almost all for pierced ears and I've never had mine pierced.

"Well let's do it here," Petra suggested. "Your uncle can afford it! You could use a haircut and manicure too. Irene hesitated and then smiled.

"You're sure it's safe? They know how to do it?"

"They know how to do everything here," said Petra. "They can upholster the car, change your rims, examine your glasses, get you drunk, get you tattooed, get you fucked, abort your brat, give you a haircut, manicure and massage, and even pierce your ears." All three of them laughed at Petra's outburst and they sought out the adequate places for Irene's transformation.

Within a couple of hours, they were back at the earing store, choosing oh so carefully. Irene was glowing, laughing with Petra like two sisters enjoying a life of crime. He ended buying two sets of earrings for each girl plus one for his sister and Irene's sister. After that, the girls wanted a beer and then they turned to tequila. Then they got hungry and wanted to eat everything in sight. He knew a special place on the road to Tecate, so they took off in that direction, stopping, eating taco after taco, and coming to the little town almost at twilight. There, stuffed and drunk, they found a group of kids playing foosball in the plaza. Petra challenged them to a game, and he stood by watching his drunk companions play game after game with the kids until they had to go home, and then the threesome entered the Diana Bar and asked for a round of tequila, and then another.

He tried to drink as little as possible and went to the bathroom trying to clear his head for the long ride home. When he came back, Irene was crying beyond consolation. She cried about her mother, her sister, her life and now her uncle who was so different from the man she'd known some years before. Soon she was crying about her haircut, her manicure, her pierced ears and even her earrings. Petra tried to console her, embrace her, but Irene would have no part of it.

"Keep away from me," she said, "You're no sister or friend of mine. You're ruining my uncle's life, but don't try to mess up mine."

He and Petra helped her out of the bar and into the car. "Let me sit in the back," she insisted, and then they helped her in the car where she continued to cry until she fell asleep as they crossed the border and cut through the mountains toward San Diego.

7.

Arriving at his apartment, Irene went to the bathroom, and he heard her throw up. Before going to bed, she knocked on his bedroom door, to tell her uncle that she would take the bus back to L.A. the next day. In the morning after coffee, he told Petra he wanted to drive Irene to L.A. When she offered to go with him, he told her, "No, it's better I spend some quality time with her."

"I could sleep in the back," she offered.

"No," he said firmly, "it's better I take her."

Miffed, she desisted in her efforts. He helped Irene pack her things and take them to the car. "I'm sorry," she said to Petra, "But this was just too much for me."

She mounted the car, and off they went. But as he made his way toward the freeway, she said, "No, Mel," dropping the "uncle" perhaps for the first time in her life. "I really want to take the bus, please try to understand." He tried to convince her, but she insisted, and he eventually took her to the bus station, bought her a ticket, waited for her departure, kissed her goodbye, and helped her on board.

"Irene I'm sorry things turned out this way, and that I wasn't there for you as much as I'd planned."

"I understand," she said, turning philosophical. "I've been an idiot too," she said, kissing him goodbye. "But I'll tell you one thing," she said. "You better get away from that girl as fast as you can."

When he got to the house, Petra had packed everything she'd had in the apartment. "What brings you back?" she asked.

"She wanted to take the bus, and I wanted to be with you, so I let her go."

"Bullshit," she said. "If she'd have wanted you to take her, you'd have left me here stranded like a whale on the shore."

"But here I am," he said.

"But not me," she said. "You and your oh so sweet and sensitive niece should really live together, but as for me, I'm out of here."

"But you tell me one thing," he insisted, surprised by her vehemence. "What happened between you two in the Diana Bar?"

"I don't know what you're talking about," she said, piling up her things at the door.

"You know damn well something happened," he said. "Because that wasn't the same girl who was with us before I walked away."

"Well, you should know by now that you should never leave a girl alone at a bar—you should never go away."

"Well?" he said, almost leaning over her.

"Well, the waitress came by and said we looked like two lovers and asked if we wanted to rent a room, and I laughed and said, yes, why not? And I asked her how much! And then your goody-two-shoes niece started crying and farting, and all the things you saw when you came back from the can."

He just stared at her. "And that's what you said to my niece?"

"That's right, and why not, she was kinda cute and drunk, and it might've been good for her. I know I would have had a good time."

"Thanks a lot," he said. "But I think you're right—it's a good time to move out."

And with that he lifted her things up and helped her out the door, ready to put them in his car. "Don't bother," she said, "I already called a cab." And like magic, the cab arrived. The driver helped her load the cab, and opened the door for her to get in. Once settled, she rolled down the window. "Well, sweetie, I hope you like your weekends without me, I hope you like screwing your pillow as much as you liked making love to me."

8.

He passed many a lonely weekend, many days without Petra in his life; and the more time he spent alone or even with other women, the more he missed this young Jewish Dutch girl who called him "sweetie" and "honey" and made him feel better than he had in years. He thought of her life, her actions, and knew she was outrageous and impossible, but he missed her all the more.

One night she called him to see how he was doing, she claimed. "You miss me, don't you?" she would say, "Just as I said you would."

"Yes," he admitted.

"You want me to come over," she said, not asked. And he confirmed, yes, and then she'd say, "But you know I shouldn't, right? Because you know I'm wrong for you and you for me."

"Yes," he would admit sadly. And she kissed him through the phone.

"Good night sweetie, happy dreams."

She called him a few times like this during the next few months. And he answered much as he always did, always wishing she'd come to his apartment, so he could kiss her again, tongue her and feel and listen as she came in his mouth, with her immersed in some fantasy he was all too eager to imagine. Then more than a month passed without a call. He was with another woman when he heard the phone ring.

"Hi, honey," she said. Self-conscious because of his guest, he answered rather curtly.

"What's up?" he asked; and she told him that she'd met a young man her own age at the campus cafeteria where they both were working, that he'd just received an offer to manage a cafeteria at a small college in Oregon, and that he asked her if she'd go with him, to work with him and—guess what—to be his wife. And she'd decided—why not? She had nothing holding her since he'd stopped loving her. She decided it was time to try to make a new life after all she'd been through. And so yes, she was going to marry him and what's more, she wanted Mel to be at the wedding and, in fact, give her away.

He remained silent, digesting her news, not knowing what to say. And then he knew he was hurt and angry beyond words.

"You mean you're going to turn me down?" she asked, almost weeping in her voice.

"But who is this kid?" he answered. "You're making a stupid choice. I love you and I want you to be with me."

"But I love him and I'm going with him."

"But can you be faithful to him?"

"Maybe not," she answered, "but I'd never been faithful to you either if you must know." And then she asked once again, "Are you going to come to the wedding, or aren't you? Are you going to be there to wish me well and give me away?"

And he wanted to answer from the bottom of his rancor and sense of loss, to find a way to hurt this girl he'd never wanted and now wanted more than he could have imagined.

"So, you want me to come so I can see you do what you'll see will break my heart," he said.

"Don't be a baby, sweetie. You know I can't invite my father, and you're the only one I want, because I love you," she said. And she began to cry; and try as he might, and as angry as he was for her playing him so well, he could not refuse her.

"Don't cry," he said. "I'll be there and do all you want, and I'll see you leave my life with tears in my eyes, but I'll do it." She thanked him, laughing softly, telling him she was so happy and that she loved him so.

"But I have a condition," he said.

"What's that?"

"I want to invite Irene. I'm not sure she'll come but I want to invite her."

"Yes," she said, "It'll be great to see her again, and ask her to forgive me."

And so it was. And it was all very fine, even though Irene declined the invitation. After the wedding was over, he kissed Petra one last time, feeling some sense of fulfillment, but also a sense of loss and pain, knowing all too well that her marriage would probably fail. However, whether it did or not, he knew he was never to see her or hear from her again.

The Wig

1.

Bald at twenty-four, Mel had never thought about it too much. It was an impediment to pleasure but not happiness, he thought. He had probably spent more nights alone than he would have liked to consider because of it, but each of us had a cross—indeed many crosses—and this one was one of his. Of course, it bothered him when he went out and women declined to dance with him. But that may have been because he was a terrible dancer, or because he was shy—though maybe he was shy because he was a terrible dancer or ... because he was bald.

Maybe all this explained some of his most unhappy moments in high school, when a particularly annoying friend would see him from above on the staircase—"Mel, your spot's as a big as a quarter." "Mel, it's a fifty-cent piece," he mocked. "You're heading for the silver dollar!"

Then there was the girl he was crazy about, who put her hands in his hair, only to feel the bald spot. "My gosh," she said, amazed; and she soon stopped answering his calls.

Maybe it explained the lack of dates or the tentative relationships with one girl or another. Maybe it even explained his terrible first marriage—perhaps it was that bald men couldn't be choosy in picking their mates—as well as the weekend after countless weekend he spent alone after his separation and divorce. He simply couldn't hook up with anyone, and he lived each day in misery, unable to produce, unable at times to breathe. Maybe his baldness explained his ever-recurrent sense of inferiority, his impoverished sense of worth and well-being. Maybe it at least helped explain his deep depression and despondence.

154

To be sure, it was a family thing—his father and his father's brothers were all bald, all with that same horrendous friar's fringe that seemed to turn off so many women. But somehow Mel was the one who couldn't cope with it, who lived in misery. At first, he tried to find a cure, went to several specialists, but they said his case could only be corrected by extended and expensive treatments. He tried some of them, but the results were poor. Soon he gave up and accepted his fate and its effect on every aspect of his life. Not that he lived with a full consciousness of the problem. And indeed, he contributed to it immensely by compulsively pulling out his own thinning and weakened hairs. It was as if he said to himself, I'm doomed to baldness, and so be it. I shall even embrace the process, help the baldness along. Still, he acted as if he were still in the race, as if nothing were different about him, as if there were no laws that applied to the question of his baldhead. His other problem, his weight and his struggle to keep it down, was more central to his life and action. But with this problem resolved at least temporarily by the weight loss induced by his divorce, the key issue in Mel's life had to be his baldness, and then his wig, and then how to get rid of that same wig when the time to do so came and then almost went.

2.

It was not he who had thought about getting a wig, but rather one of the least probable women with whom he'd had an affair during his period of divorce in the late 1960s. Mel was becoming involved in anti-war demonstrations, he grew a beard and moustache, eventually getting rid of the beard to express his then relatively moderate position even as he started going to and holding assorted antiwar fundraisers and participating in rallies as the decade heated up. His intellectual and cultural interests were fairly broad, sending him to art openings, theater performances and symphony concerts, but also to African American and, increasingly, Latino events, even reaching the point that he was starting to speak Spanish with some fluency and to reach out toward Latinas as his

155

principal dates. His circle of friends and lover candidates stemmed from these outreach efforts. However, this improbable woman friend came from his great passion for jazz and the groupies who hung around the musicians.

Anne was a groupie, and groupies rarely clicked with each other; if they did, their romance was usually brief and perhaps unimpassioned. They met at a jazz club through their mutual friend, Aldo Park, a saxophone player and schoolteacher as good-looking as Mel was not, who, with his ex-wife and Mel's, for a while made up a foursome until the two men discovered that the two women were having an affair and were embarked on extended lesbian explorations that grew more intense and finally led to the rupture of both marriages. Aldo and he always joked painfully about their shared sense of betrayal and humiliation, with Mel more than once commenting that women seemed to prefer lovers who weren't bald. Anne seemed different, for she had had a brief affair with Aldo and then a bald musician, and now seemed ready to try out her fellow jazz groupie. They talked some local and international jazz talk, went to an after-hours party, and ended up sharing her bed on a rainy San Diego night. They started dating, often eating out, and even going to a movie once or twice, but their great passion were the sadly deficient jazz clubs of San Diego of those long-ago years.

Aldo's friend Ronnie, a black singer, dancer, and comic, sometimes performed at the jazz clubs and other venues, sometimes with Aldo and sometimes without. Mel and his new girlfriend became almost regulars, going to Ronnie's events, and sometimes dancing as he sang. Ronnie was totally bald, and he always called out from the bandstand to Mel, "Hey brother baldy, glad you could make it!"

Mel was not too happy with the greeting but accepted it as best he could. But Anne sensed it. "Don't let him get to you," she said. "He just hates being bald and wants a whitey to suffer for it."

Mel's dancing was certainly bad, and his hypersensitivity made things worse. He was also poor and couldn't provide Anne the fancy meals and gifts she usually expected from a man she was sleeping with. It was never an exclusive or intense relationship anyway. But things began to fade when Mel invited her for a weekend in San Felipe, down the coast a hundred miles south of Mexicali, where they stayed, as he'd planned, not in a beachfront hotel, but in the back of his station wagon on a tent and trailer-lined beach. One night was more than enough, she said, complaining of a sore back, and saying she'd never experienced something so awful in her life.

Back in the city, his thirtieth birthday coming up, Ann called him and took him for what she mysteriously called his special birthday treat—a trip to a specialist who began fitting him for a hairpiece. "This is going to be my gift to you," she said.

"But I don't want a wig," he said.

"It's a hairpiece," she insisted. "You think you don't one, but this is going to change your life and you'll never regret it." He was flattered as she coaxed into the fitting, and into the consultation he received about how to fix and maintain the hairpiece that had already been designed according to his specifications. The date was set, and they met again to put it on and receive final corrections and instructions. Anne paid the final bill, and they left the specialist, Mel's wig in place, for a special birthday lunch at their favorite jazz cafe.

"Now you have your hairpiece, and now you'll have more luck with more suitable women. Our time's over," she said, getting up from the table, and gathering her things. "No," she said, "you have your lunch—don't worry, I paid for it. We had fun, but it really had to end. Have a great birthday and great life," she said. "And don't eat too much," she added, kissing him on the cheek and leaving him speechless as she walked out the door.

3.

Mel was crushed. He knew the relationship would have to end sooner or later, but why on this special day—his thirtieth birthday when his whole life was in the balance? Why a wig which seemed a total repudiation of the simple and honest life he had been trying to live, despite failure on failure? His thirtieth birthday—he'd be damned if he'd spend the night alone. But what could he do? He had backburnered the other women circulating around him since he took up with Anne. Most of them would be with current loves and none of them would appreciate a last-minute call. Then he remembered an older woman, maybe some forty-five years old, who had invited him to have a drink with her any Saturday night he wished at a bar she always frequented. He knew only she would know him at that bar and that he could try his new headgear there with her.

Arriving at about ten o'clock, he looked around for the woman and there she was, her peroxided blonde hair not hard to find in the biggest crowd. He walked up to her and sat down in the empty stool right next to her. "So," he said, "are you going to buy me a drink?" She looked at him and smiled. She was really happy to see him, she said, purposefully making her interest in him rather obvious and indicating with a slight slur and much enthusiasm that she had already been drinking for some time.

"Matt, this is my friend, Mel," she told the bartender. He ordered a double vodka and seven, and she said, "That's great, I'll have one too—put it on my tab." Then she looked at Mel again for a second; a puzzled look crossed her face, and then she burst out laughing. "I can't believe it!" she exclaimed. "I didn't even notice at first. I just knew somehow you looked different."

"Do I look weird?" he asked. "Would that be the right word?"

"No," she said, "you look great—fabulous honey. You look so much younger—you should've done it years ago," she said, running her fingers through his hairpiece. "Ooh, it almost feels real! We should really get one on to celebrate your new life!" she said, starting on her drink

"Not a bad idea," he agreed, taking a large swig of his. "Especially since tonight is my 30th," he told her.

"No!" she said, "and you're here with li'l ol' me."

"Couldn't think of any one nicer to spend it with," he said, drinking again.

"Matt, another round," she called out, startling a few people down the bar. "Well, this is something we've got to celebrate— we'll make it a memorable occasion," she said, touching his hairpiece again, laughing and then giving him a long and probing kiss.

It all went as he had hoped, his car following hers to her apartment, making love to her in the most excited and desperate way. They both came and enjoyed, smoked cigarettes, and eventually said goodbye as the sun rose. "Have a breakfast date," she said. "The party's over."

"It was a blast," he said.

"Don't wait too long to call me," she said, kissing him on the check.

"Don't worry," he said, knowing he would probably never call no matter how grateful he was, no matter how good the night had been.

4.

When he got home, he took off the wig and looked at himself. Then he put it on and looked again. On the one hand, he realized how much younger he looked in the wig, how much more attractive he might be for a woman who was not aware he was wearing it. Even his woman friend had been fascinated by it, had touched his head lovingly and probably at that moment decided for sure she would have him.

On the other hand, he couldn't help but think how impossible the gift was. He certainly didn't plan to teach his classes or see any of his colleagues in his new hairpiece. He certainly wasn't going to the jazz clubs or Latino events he frequented with the wig on his head. When and how would he ever use this absurd, ridiculous gift?

But then he realized he had a solution. He was traveling to Mexico again this summer to study Spanish and get ready for the doctoral program he would enter. That would be the solution—he'd wear the wig in Mexico and then, if he got used to it, he'd keep wearing it when he took on his work as student and Teaching Assistant in the fall.

In the meantime, completely on the loose again, he could try it out with on a few of the women in his circle that he had left to their own devices while he'd pursued his relationship with Anne. He called up Myra, a former love he still had feelings for, and asked her if she was doing anything Sunday night. But though she said she wasn't, she also indicated that her new boyfriend might not like her going out with him. He called Luisa and she was tied up, though she'd love to see him some other time. Finally, he called Jill and she was free right now and very happy to receive him for coffee in her apartment. Off he went, and sure enough she laughed but was also thrilled with his wig and offered herself up like a piece of cake, continuing his thirtieth birthday party through the second day of the new phase of his life.

A few days later, Mayra called and said Jill had told her about the hairpiece and she had to see it. So he met her and she laughed, but invited him back to her place. "What about the new boyfriend?"

"Don't worry about him—besides I just made him up," she said. "Who do you like better, me or Luisa?"

"You," he said, not lying. "I was pretty crazy about you when you dumped me." "Yes," she said, "but that was because you didn't take me seriously."

"But you told me you didn't want anything serious."

"But that doesn't mean I didn't want you to want me all the way."

"Agh!" he said, "And now what?"

"We can try again," she said, running her hands through his hairpiece.

Finally, Luisa called and made passionate love with him during a long afternoon. She stroked his head, saying "I can't believe the difference it makes—it's stupid, I don't really approve of it, but I can't resist it."

Jill called again and told him Mayra had told her about sleeping with Mel. "You love her more than me," she complained.

"No, it's not true," Mel said, and went over to see her. Almost immediately they were in bed together, and so it went.

Afterwards, she continued complaining, "That was fine, but I know you really want Mayra."

Mel did his best to reassure her, but his confidence and arrogance had been growing and now he couldn't resist finally saying to her what he had wanted to say to so many others. "It's wonderful to be with you," he said, "But I guess I have to confess I'm dying to fulfill my fantasy and be in bed with you and Mayra."

Jill looked scandalized, but then said, "Well, we could try, but I'm afraid you'll just reveal how much more you want her than me."

It seemed that it was one after another, as curiosity led to erotic exploration; and it was as if Anne had given him a magic potion that made all things possible. Certainly, life was very different, happy, and orgasmic. Mel began to value his hairpiece, sometimes putting it on and staring in the mirror, shifting his head this way and that, helping himself with another mirror to catch himself and the wig from angle to angle. "What can't I do?" he asked, with growing arrogance, looking forward to the ménage-a-trois of which he had always dreamed.

And indeed, it came to pass. The two women invited him to dinner and shared out the two bottles he had brought with him. Then, drunk enough to have an excuse, they retired to the bedroom and lay down on the large bed, cuddling, kissing and laughing and then getting into it, him entering one woman and going down on the other, tonguing the clitoris of one, and even managing to touch the clitoris of the one he entered; and then switching positions, angles and roles, with the women stroking his hairpiece, with him piling up condoms (he had come well prepared only to find they had too), with them kissing him wherever they could, him sometimes arranging that the two also kissed and touched each other until the three of them came to sweet orgasm.

Afterwards, returning home, he took off the hairpiece, stared at it again, and even kissed it. He even kissed a photo he had of Anne, thanking her for his new-found happiness and joy in life.

But still, he knew that he could not wear the wig day-to-day; and his first adventures behind him, he prepared for his summer off in Mexico. Just before he left, Mayra called to say she was sure he loved Jill more than her; then Jill called to say the same about Mayra. He tried to reassure both women, who insisted on being dealt with in person.

Finally, Luisa called to complain. "I know you had a ménage a trois with Mayra and Jill, I feel so rejected," she said, "and now I hear you're leaving for Mexico."

162

"But don't worry, Luisa," he answered, "I would have loved it if you had been with us, and I'm sure we can cook up something when I come back."

"Don't lose the wig," she said, "And have as many affairs as you can in Mexico. In fact, I won't go to bed with you alone or with two or three other women, unless you tell me about making love to at least ten women on your trip."

5.

Mel left the next day with clear aspirations: to give his wig a chance, learn how to clean it, paste it, and groom it, and use it to meet and seduce a significant number of women. As in prior trips, he crossed the border in Mexicali, and then moved on to San Luis de Colorado, to Hermosillo, to Guaymas, Ciudad Obregón, Navojoa, Los Mochis, Culiacán, and finally Mazatlán.

It was in San Luis that he had his first encounter, an easy touch with an older woman in a bar with hardly any lights. Mel's second came in Bahía Kino, where he latched on to a waitress who made love with him on the beach while her young boy slept in the station wagon, wetting the mattress during the night, so that in the morning Mel, ever more callous, mean, and self-centered with his new wig, berated mother and son and abandoned them both as he drove off unencumbered on his way to Mazatlán.

It was in this key resort town, the site of his sad honeymoon some years before that he intended to fully undertake his great experiment. He checked into the main hotel along the old beach front, and then prepared his wig with great care, taping it on and going through his grooming instructions. Each day he went to the beach and swam with his wig; each day he cleaned and groomed it; then in the night he would explore the city's coastal nightclub world, observing how the young locals latched on to the secretaries and nurses just off the plane from L.A. or Phoenix. Soon enough, he began his whirl, talking to one woman and then another, trying

163

out different lines and having a share of success far beyond what he had had in his wigless days. One night he met a slim young woman just off the L.A. shuttle; and in less than an hour, he was making love to her in the back of his station wagon. At one point she put her hand on his head and broke her rhythm toward orgasm, while he confessed that he was wearing a hairpiece.

"But you don't need it," she said, still panting, and kissing him again and again.

"I'm pretty sure you wouldn't be here if you'd met me without it."

"That isn't so," she said, sucking on his tongue and returning to her vacation pleasure.

"Oh yes, it is," he said, as they both reached the conclusion of their workout.

The next day they woke up, went to breakfast, and realized that they wanted to continue being together during her days in Mexico. Suddenly her initial plans went to the four winds, as they took the long, winding road to Durango and then on to one place after another, making love more than once almost every day, with him wondering how to count all these fine times in relation to the requisites laid out by Luisa. Did she insist on ten different encounters—if so, he'd almost met the goal—or ten different partners? If the latter wer so, he would have to wait until his new friend took off on her return flight. In fact, as the days passed, he became more anxious for her departure and began to regret the power of the hairpiece that had made this new relationship possible. It was not that he liked her less, but it began to bother him that every daily pleasure and every nightly orgasm with her was due to something so superficial as his wig-based transformation. Finally, the day came, and he took her to the airport, where they kissed goodbye promising to get together on his return, though in truth, he knew he would never see her again.

So now began his true time in Mexico, as he traveled from encounter to encounter, in town after town; and in almost each instance, with the help of his wig (so he believed), his charmed life continued. He even managed to advance fully in his Spanish through his many flings and more extended summer adventures, so that in a sense he would forever owe his Spanish and whatever academic and personal success he might have in the future, in part at least, to Ann's gift.

Nevertheless, the exhilaration he had first felt with his first encounters with the wig continued to fade. Quite glibly, and against the logic of a whole series of feminist texts that were now appearing almost daily, Mel came to believe that most women were almost as superficial in their sources of attraction as were men. How else explain the impact of his hairpiece? How else explain its allure, its magic? He gradually started to resent its power and the very women who apparently fell under its spell; he began to resist the arrogant and yes machistic personality he had been developing under the spell of the wig. He even became jealous of the wig, realizing that his hairpiece and not he himself was the source of his apparent attraction.

One way he expressed his new negativity was to neglect grooming the wig properly. It soon bleached under the Mexican sun, and his efforts to dye and re-dye it, to keep it clean of sand and dirt, were a constant problem. First meticulous in his efforts, he soon followed his general tendencies toward sloppiness and negligence. And his depression grew with each new wig romance and each day as his Mexican hiatus came to an end.

6.

By the time he came back to San Diego in the last days of summer, he was so depressed and demoralized by his wig, that he didn't even bother to look for the girlfriends with whom he had played in the days before his departure; he never called Luisa, never had his well-earned ménage-à-trois. In a terrible funk, he moved into a new apartment and began taking all the steps needed to launch a new phase of his life, as he entered a program of Literature doctoral studies.

But here, he faced a crucial fork in his road. For as he readied himself for his first day of classes, he had to decide whether he should wear the wig or not. He knew what the decision should be. But then, he was terribly afraid of facing the student ordeal before him alone. And without the wig, he knew he'd be alone, facing long days and nights without any love partner, facing his advancing age with the fear of perpetual loneliness. For a moment, the superficial quality of his wigged love affairs seemed of less importance than it had during the summer.

"Better a superficial relationship than none at all," he reasoned stupidly, driven by his fears. "And who knows?" he heard a devilish voice inside him (or was it on his head?) say, "Maybe you'll have better luck now. You shouldn't give up your wig—it's brought you pleasure and happy nights, the only happiness you've had." And indeed, it was not easy to just abandon the very cause of whatever small happiness he had known in recent days. And so, in this moment of colossal weakness, disregarding the context and consequences that would mark this decision, he made the terrible mistake of deciding to wear it.

Nothing could have been more unsuitable than a hair-pieced graduate student in the last year of the 60s. What could have been more ridiculous than this silly man who claimed to be a contemporary literary student and yet wore a wig to class? All the magic that the wig possessed in the spring dissipated now, leaving

166

no residue. Just as women were drawn to him in the first place, now they seemed repelled. The very wig that had won him so many pleasurable hours now offered him a fuller sense of loneliness and emptiness than he had known in years.

And now the enormity of his error came upon him; for once starting his new student days with the wig, how was he to take it off? How could he have underestimated this problem? It was a matter of pride and of course the fear of humiliation, for no matter how embarrassing it was to wear the wig, no matter how many negative things his peers might be whispering about him, the more humiliating it seemed to submit to their pressures, do away with the wig and incite their snide jokes and jeers. Something stubborn and destructive grew in him, and he resisted every impulse to rid himself of what had become his curse. And meanwhile the wig became more insistent, demanding that he give it more time, groom it as he had done before, treat it with the love it deserved and required. And the more the wig demanded, the more depressed and hostile he became, actually repeating what he had done in his youth with his balding head, actually pulling hairs from it one by one until indeed, he had to begin to brush his wig hairs this way and that to hide bald spots on the headpiece itself, and push it somewhat back on his head to make sure that it did not leave a bald space between his remaining fringe and the hairless part of his head. And yet these maneuvers made him only angrier and more resentful of his wig and indeed his fellow students who he felt were holding back their urge to laugh when they saw him in that ever more disheveled and ridiculous *thing* he had on his head.

Meanwhile the situation on campus grew more intense over the war in Cambodia and actual killings of student demonstrators at other universities. A student burned himself alive on his own campus, and Mel's earlier political instincts reasserted themselves as he began participating in rallies and marches. The reemergence of his politics led to his closer contacts and friendships with students of similar convictions and commitments. He began to attend political meetings and actually spoke up and participated in group decisions. His politics carried over to the classroom where he found himself taking radical political stances on literary matters, whether he was discussing Sophocles or Euripides, Beckett or Brecht.

Things became so heated that the wig became intolerable and his war with it escalated, as did the war in Vietnam. But he still didn't have the inner strength to throw it off and seek to end its declining but still obvious power over his being. The situation grew worse as his relations with new friends grew closer, and even as he began to feel the tug of a possible relationship with one of the Latina women among them.

He came to the point where he took his new woman friend for a coffee ostensibly to talk politics and studies, and really to see if this were someone with whom he should pursue a relationship. During their conversation, Mel had the courage to ask her out on a date. And she took his hand and told him. "I'd love to, Mel, but let me tell you, I just wouldn't think of going out with you until you do something about your ridiculous wig."

Mel felt his face flush. He had had no overt discussion about his hairpiece with anyone, and stupidly, the first thing he said in answer was just this. "It's called a hairpiece."

"Well, let me tell you," she said, "It's absurd, it demeans you, it's the one thing that makes your new friends question everything you do—all of us. Someone so smart and committed and so stuck in a web of bourgeois appearances."

"Very good," he said, impressed by her class analysis. "But the fact is I owe my recent happiness and pleasures to my hairpiece," he went on, for some reason defending a position in which he no longer believed.

"Then maybe you should date your wig—excuse me, your hairpiece—and not me."

"Listen," he said, "it's not as easy to get rid of as you think. It would be so embarrassing."

"Why," she asked. "Everyone knows you're wearing the thing, and you groom it so poorly, it's often not in place, and needs reconstruction. Everyone knows, so why don't you just get rid of it?"

"I can't," he said, almost trembling with frustration. "I know they know, and I know they know I know. But I just can't subject myself to the humiliation of letting them know I know they know and giving them the satisfaction of pressuring me out of it."

"But it's humiliating to wear it when you know we all know and when you even agree with us that you shouldn't wear it."

"I just can't explain it," he said, "but I just can't do it. I know I've got to do something, but I have to work this out myself."

"Listen," she said, "you're not alone in this, we're willing to help, I'm willing to help, but you've got to work this out."

"I'll try," he said, and went his sad, lonely way.

7.

Mel was now in full crisis. He genuinely liked this woman, her frankness and gravity, he even liked the low timber of her voice, her Spanish accent and her bedroom eyes so evident in the midst of her most political or intellectual endeavors. But the wig still had him, and he still didn't know how to get rid of this terrible addiction that was now destroying the only chance for happiness he had before him.

Very quickly a possible solution presented itself. He was taking a course in surrealism team-taught by two famous professors. His own presentation was to be on *hazard objectif*, *humour noir*, *amour fou* and *cruauté*—key terms in the surrealist revolutionary arsenal. He wrote his paper with great enthusiasm but also fear, anticipating the opinions of his professors and their inner circle of

169

loyal and intensely competitive students. He was impressed by his own ideas for the paper; but then, insecure about its effect, it occurred to him he could end his presentation with a bang, by throwing his wig on the table in an act of daring and bravura. With great trepidation, he made his way to the seminar and set forth his presentation. As he came to an end, he drew his hands to his head, ready, he thought, to rip the tape from his skull and throw the wig across the seminar table in the direction of his professors. But before he could do this, one of the students began making violent objections to his paper, raising one issue after another, and showing off his superior understanding of surrealist principles than could this novice and wigged fellow student. Mel felt compelled to defend his positions, and his opportunity passed as he sensed that his planned gesture would mark an intellectual defeat as if he was seeking extreme theatricality to distract from the weakness of his arguments.

The next day, he told his woman friend about what happened, and she was not very consoling. "That just shows your weakness, Mel. No matter how good your paper might have been, you let this student and yes, your damned wig, control you, when the real point of surrealism is freedom and revolution. Where's your integrity? Where are your politics?"

8.

Mel could not deny her logic. He was even more intent on throwing off his hairpiece and pursuing a woman who had such a sense of purpose and gravity and perhaps offered him a means of getting and keeping his feet on the ground. But his big chance missed, what could he do to resolve his problem? Getting rid of the hairpiece was not immediately possible, but short of that what could be done? And then finally he began to think strategically and set forth on a campaign that would lead him to the required result with the minimum amount of pain or embarrassment.

The first step was to buy a hat—and one that would fit with his developing campus role and life. So he crossed the border one more time and found a store in Tijuana where he could buy two very fine Basque *boinas*, or berets, one black and another a deep red. So, on top of his shoddy, depillidated hairpiece, he placed the black boina for everyday use and the red one for the demonstrations in which he participated. The desired effect was achieved, as his fellow students complimented him on his new style and, although he knew their implicit meaning with respect to his wig, he could act blithely, as if there were nothing more to say. At the demonstrations, the boina made him look more revolutionary, more like Che. Even his woman friend smiled and said, "what a nice idea!"

Encouraged, Mel took the next step. He stopped shaving and let his beard grow out, daily watching its growth and gradually shaping a handsome beard that he hoped would displace interest from his head to his chin. Again, there seemed an air of approval about his new transformation, as he marched and rallied in his red boina and new beard, a true son of Cuba's revolution. The semester ending and Christmas upon him, again Mel crossed the border, buying two more boinas and this time going to a barber, who did as he requested—shaving his head completely.

"Yul Brynner," said the barber, happy with his work. But this was no imitation of the actor who had made bald men seem so appealing and sexy to a generation of women. Mel retained his growing beard, grooming it until it reached its rounded guerrillero glory. So it was when he returned to campus for the winter semester, that a new revolutionary Mel emerged, replete with beard, boina and bald head.

The transformation was complete when, some weeks later, his bald head growing out of his fringe, he finally took off his boina before participating in a heated confrontation with the military at a depot where new troops were being shipped out to Vietnam. No one had time to comment or joke about the new turn in Mel's appearance. The emergence of his bald head went without comment, although (did he imagine it?) he did spy what he interpreted as a smile from his woman friend. But the fact was, the demonstration turned violent as soldiers moved against the students impeding the troop boarding. Mel joined the front lines of the protest, his bald head glistening in the bright sun as he and other students broke ranks and ran in retreat from the soldiers' aggressive advance, receiving, as did other heads bald or otherwise, ringing blows from the enraged soldiers.

Mel returned home to nurse his sore head. He knew the wig and boina would have offered him some protection, but he had survived the danger and was very satisfied at his efforts and achievement. He was proud about how he had faced his obsession and found a creative way to deal with it; he was proud of the bump on his bald head he had received for his efforts. He looked at his wig, and it was now reduced to a sad rag version of its former glorious self. He playfully placed it on his head, trying one angle or another. He took it off and wrapped it in a little bag. A few days later, he took the wig to a store and bought some flowers and a greeting card, writing a note on the card, "Here it is," he wrote. "I was wondering if we might be able to go out soon."

He put the card in an envelope and the envelope and the wig itself in the papers wrapping the flowers. He took them to his friend's apartment and knocked on the door. Her roommate answered to tell him she wasn't home—that she had left town for fear of being apprehended for her part in the demonstration. Mel offered to leave his package with the friend, who then told him, "I hope you're ok with this, but she went off with her boyfriend—they left together a few days ago, and I don't think they'll be back in town for another week."

Mel decided not to leave the package. He left the house, package in hand. Passing a garbage pail, he opened it, and tossed in his package, pausing only slightly before he closed the lid.

172

Unhappily he returned to his apartment, to face his doctoral work alone. His unhappiness grew to a state of dismay when he found out that his woman friend's friend was the fellow student who had most criticized his surrealism paper—a student, he remembered not without resentment, who sported an abundant head of unkempt and bushy hair much in keeping with the revolutionary fashions of the time. On finding this out, Mel shaved his beard, put his shaved hair and his boinas in a bag, and threw them in another garbage pail. The he began preparations for his next seminar assignment, not giving up his new politics really, still proudly wearing the rally bump on his bald head as a kind of badge of courage and defiance, but now sadder though hopefully wiser from his experience with women and his wig.

Norma and the Tender Deceit

Cut adrift from most of his post-divorce ties, Mel attended a party to which his friend Gene Schiller and his Chicana wife Veronica invited him in their San Diego home. There, he met a beautiful young Mexican friend of Veronica, Norma Caldero, and managed to get her telephone number before she left the party to go meet some friends.

Norma was very Mexican, speaking English with the thickest accent and clearly preferring to speak in Spanish. Mel was enchanted, savoring every word of their first conversation. She also had something stylish about her, wearing a sleek violet dress, her long auburn hair turned up so she seemed to have a short bob, as if her femininity were something she could unfurl like her hair. She wore makeup, covering a few pock marks, but she was so elegant, so ladylike in the most conventional but attractive way, and she made charming, flirtatious jokes about everything so that Mel felt a fire growing within him when he looked at her. But he didn't wish to repeat his errors with past mexicanas and Chicanas—with so many others. This girl seemed so much more conservative, so much more safe and also lovely, the perfect mate for a battered warrior so weary from so many battles lost. The fact that he was bald and short didn't seem to deter her; he felt the power of her attention and interest. The fact that she was a shop girl from the Lerner Store on San Diego's uninspiring Broadway only made her seem all the more suitable.

Returning home to his lonely, divorced man's cave, he thought about her; and, while trying to hold off and not show himself as over-interested, he suffered through two nights waiting for the right time to call. Doing so, he was extremely nervous, and barely found the courage to get beyond the how are you's. She indeed had to help him, laughing and saying, "*Pero, Mel, me has llamado solamente para platicar?* ... You only call me to make

174

small talk?" she repeated in English. So that finally he asked her out, and she laughed and said she would be honored to go out with such a handsome and educated professor. It was she really who set the date and time, and told him, "I'm a cheap date, because I'm watching my line." Mel thought he was clever telling her not to worry because he would watch her line for her. "Men like me because I'm such a cheap date," she told him. "But don't think I'll be paying on the first time out."

He drove up to her house in the barrio and greeted her at the door. There she was totally beautiful, her hair up in a the most graceful bun, crowned by the whitest gardenia, her breathtaking white dress cut to cover her right shoulder and then incline down toward just under her left arm, gleaming under the streetlight and then by the light of the oh so slivery moon. Mel asked her if she wanted to go to a fine restaurant in Tijuana, only to find out that she could not cross the border by any stretch of the imagination. So he took her to his favorite Lebanese bistro in a house on Fifth Street and then to a night club on top of one of San Diego's tallest buildings, where they drank as a jazz group featuring his friend Aldo set up to play. Play they did, but with music that, Mel was happy to find, was not quite danceable. She sat seemingly in rapture looking marvelous, the ideal bride-wife to his Latinized eyes, listening to the musicians and agreeing when he said the group was fine.

After the set, Aldo, still hurting from his own recent divorce from his reckless Panamanian wife, came over and sat with them for a time, speaking some Spanish to Norma, but being careful not to seem to be moving in on Mel's date. Afterwards, Mel took Norma back to her home acting in the most conservative way, feeling she was not the kind of woman to rush, no matter how great and growing his desire to bed and couple with her.

"You're not even going to kiss me?" she asked, apparently surprised by his lack of aggressivity.

"I don't want to rush things. You're just too beautiful and I'm almost falling in love with you already."

"Then you must kiss me," she said. "I came out with you because I felt an attraction. We need to explore it a little, don't you think?"

She therefore kissed him, caressed the nape of his neck, and responded to his reciprocal moves and the small advances he signaled, with his lips and tongue. Soon he was completely enthralled and could think of nothing but losing himself in her.

"Maybe we should go to my place," he said. But she then withdrew her body just a bit, moved away from him on the seat just a bit, and the moment faded.

"I think we should think about this a little bit," she said, "But yes, you excite me and make me want to do more than I know I should. Call me," she said, getting out of his car.

Each time he spoke to Norma on the phone, she was pleasant enough. But it was clear she was in retreat. When he finally pressed her, she confessed she'd been seeing someone else and that the whole startup with him had been a test run to see if she was really ready to move on. However, as much as she had enjoyed their encounter, and had felt urgings to be with him, still she couldn't get herself to bite the bullet. Mel felt wounded, put down and embittered once again. He tried to reason with himself that she was the wrong woman for him, that he should not pursue this relationship, that he was lucky she hadn't played him along on a string until he was completely and hopelessly captured by her. As time passed, their phone talks grew fewer, as she obviously remained with her boyfriend, and he began to pursue other women on the border playing field.

A year or so later, Mel got involved in a relationship with another Latina woman, who would indeed become his second wife. And strangely, in the course of a conversation with Ariana, his

176

mother-in-law to be, he suddenly realized that mother and daughter both knew Norma and that Ariana actually had business dealings with her even more than with other downtown San Diego shop girls—almost on a weekly basis. Mel owned up to having dated her once, and Ariana said, "Well then you're the one."

"What do you mean?" Mel asked.

"You're the Jewish man she dated just when she realized she was pregnant by another man. You're the one she thought of seducing into a fake fatherhood and a marriage—and even getting her papers; and then she realized she liked you too much to do it and just broke off with you."

Mel was completely taken aback and went so far as to wonder if Norma's billowing white dress might have been hiding a belly that was starting to swell. But Ariana laughed.

"The truth is I asked her if you were rich, and she told me she didn't think so, so I told her she should marry for love—but only with someone who was rich or had the potential to be so. And I also told her a not very good-looking Jew without money was no great catch, even if at least he could never accuse her of marrying him for his money."

"So maybe you saved my life," Mel suggested.

"Or maybe I saved you for my daughter. Latina women are very tricky," Ariana told him.

"Are you talking about Norma or your daughter?" Mel asked.

"All of us," she answered. "Especially me!" she said laughing. "But Norma, she was a good girl, as poor as could be, and with a poor boyfriend who probably didn't care for her any way. And there were you, a gringo hope on her horizon, as fat, bald, ugly and Jewish as you are, and she decided she cared for you too much to take advantage of you."

Mel realized how far his illusions were from his realities and wondered where his love for Latinas might lead. He also wondered what had happened to beautiful Norma. Her choosing to spare him from an illusion of fatherhood and love indeed made him long to be with her and want to find her, to love her all the more. He was overwhelmed by the thought that this lovely woman had rejected him not because she didn't care for him but because she did.

"So what's happened to her?" he asked Ariana.

"Ah, she had her baby, but the father disappeared and her aunt invited her back to Michoacán, and I haven't heard from her or seen her for months, so I guess she took her baby and went back to *el rancho grande* or maybe even *chico*. Who knows?"

III. Goodbyes to the Border

The Point of No Return

In all his deepening relation with Mexican/U.S. border worlds, Mel had tended to see less of his parents while he spent more and more of his time on the southern side of the border. His growing Spanish and then his growing obsession with the border, with Latinos and all things Latin American seemed a matter of strange life choices and indeed radical distortions of the paths Jewish sons were supposed to take in those Cold War years.

Still, he was their only son, and they continued to visit him in San Diego, happy when he announced that in all probability his terrible first marriage was coming to an end, and happy enough, at least eventually with the Nicaraguan border woman he was to marry a few years down the line. During the end of his first marriage, the two-year plus divorce period and then his new relationship and marriage, they would come down to San Diego once every few months, sometimes taking in the sights of the city, but sometimes also traveling with him across the border to Tijuana or further south.

In principle there was no problem as long as he made sure his mother ate at a Jewish deli or seafood restaurant before they crossed, and as long as the plan included some time for his father (and also his mother) to gamble at the Aguas Calientes race course or the famous Jai Alai *frontón* at the upper end of the tourist strip.

His father was quite interested in tasting all the dishes and flavors he might enjoy and seek to imitate in his catering business. But for several years, his mother had refused to try Mexican food at all. "I can drink every drink they serve except that one with a worm or if they put in some dirty ice, but the food's something you won't see me trying." So sometimes she'd sit nursing a Coke while Mel and his father would try different tacos, tortas or enchiladas. Mel would ask her if she might want some eggs or some tortillas and cheese. But she held firm.

"Even if they served Kosher meat, I wouldn't touch it," she said. Or "God knows what they cooked that in."

All of which meant that their excursions across the border tended to be brief. Because even if they ended up packing a few sandwiches before crossing the border (the great solution Mel finally dreamed up), the problem would be her phobia about the bathrooms—he just couldn't get her to try them; even in the finest places with the softest toilet paper, she just had troubles. "I just can't stand sitting down," she said, coining a phrase that stayed with Mel the rest of his life. Or when something happened that made her feel she'd reached her limit, she'd say, this was "the point of no return," and when something else horrendous happened, she'd say, Yogi Berra-style, "Here we are coming back to the same point of no return all over again."

In the midst of it all, she seemed to enjoy the border's exotic touch and even some of the shops along Avenida Revolución. In fact, a typical day with Mel would be to go to the racetrack and follow that up with a stroll down block after block of the stores (Mel steering them away from any place that was at all raunchy), Mel's father fascinated by the hawkers and the schlock merchandise, and his mother loving the more elegant stores with French perfumes and Spanish soaps. Or another typical day would be to shop in the evenings and then go to the

Only one thing was to shake up their routine, and that occurred on an evening they came over for a night of Jai Alai games that Mel remembers to this day. For some reason probably related to his confused and lonely sex life, he was in a foul mood, taking it out on his mother, complaining about her phobias which were preventing her from experiencing Mexico, telling her she had to get over all this and take a trip to Mexico City and beyond before time ran out. "You owe it to dad," he argued, "and even yourself." She gave him her usual arguments against, but Mel persisted. "I bet even

181

some synagogue in L.A. has their own cruise trip or tour with Kosher Mexican food on board."

On and on, he ragged about how knowing another country enriched one's life and how he felt so fortunate to have a country so close by and so economical that he could plan trips almost any time he was free.

"I don't know," she answered. "You don't seem so happy with all your trips. You think you know all about this place, but maybe you need to come over here less."

His father remained silent throughout this whole discussion—a man of fewer and fewer words as he grew older. "Listen," he finally said, "You think you know this little part of Mexico pretty well, right?"

"Yes," Mel answered rather tentatively, sensing something perhaps not too pleasant coming his way.

"Well, I can show you something about this shopping street that you don't know but your mother will recognize in a flash." It was then that his father proceeded to size up different stores staring at the facades.

"See this?" he said pointing to a mezuzah on the door. Then he ushered them in and went searching for the store owner.

And sure enough, he spotted an older, balding white man sitting by the cash register. He went up to him and started saying the few phrases he knew in Yiddish. And sure enough, the owner's eyes lit up and they got into an interminable conversation about how the owner's family left Russia in 1905, how they wanted to go to New York or Buenos Aires but ended up finding a sponsor in Mexico City, and then moved to Tijuana to join other family members who had already established businesses there.

On the conversation went, until my father had learned more about the city's Jewish community than Mel had ever imagined. Soon he had the address of two local synagogues, one recently started for Christian-born Mexicans, and another more regular one they could visit on their next Saturday morning in Tijuana.

"It's my son who should go there," said Mel's mother, "so he could meet a nice Spanish-speaking Jewish girl.'

"Well," the *landsman* said, "Most of the Jewish girls here speak Spanish, English and some Yiddish or ladino too."

"Perfect," his mother said. "He should have it so good," spouting her English translation of a Yiddish phrase.

"Forget about the girls," said Mel. "Let me just ask you where Jewish people here go to eat."

"Well," he said, "there's no Jewish restaurants, but there are places you can eat without worrying about lard or meat in your café con leche." And he took out a tourist map and pointed to a few restaurants, mainly in the better hotels.

And then my father said, "why don't you circle some of the Jewish-owned stores?" And the owner circled several, including some non-tourist places of business on Avenida Constitución, which paralleled the tourist street. "And why don't you add those synagogues as well," suggested Mel's mother.

By the time they left that one store, they virtually had a Jewish map of Tijuana, plus a tip for them to visit a fine French hotel and restaurant in Ensenada. "The family's not Jewish, but a lot of Baja Jews and visitors go there, and you can have a great weekend just sleeping at their hotel and their restaurant across the street."

That night they entered some of his mother's favorite stores, and she just glowed when she met the Jewish owners. She was surprised and thrilled to find that her favorite perfume and soap store was Jewish-owned, and one Jewish woman, presumably an owner, showed them her half-clandestine line of Israeli products, which his mother could not resist buying.

"We don't show them to everyone." The woman explained. "There's just too much anti-Semitism here."

It was their best night in Mexico ever, as his mother ate a meatless meal at one of the recommended restaurants and they went on to win at Jai Alai.

Mel could not help but have mixed feelings about the Jewish world his father had uncovered for him. He was happy his parents were happy, but somehow their sense of ethnic pride and solidarity rankled him, when he came to realize how fellow Jews like his parents and perhaps like him were part of the all but hidden well-to-do infrastructure of this city of *pobres*. One thing was stores on the tourist street or elsewhere. But another thing was to consider what other businesses and what other ways Jews like his parents and perhaps like him were inevitably implicated in as part of a system that might not be too favorable to the local Mexicans—to say nothing of the city or the country as a whole.

Even while thinking such thoughts, however, he could not but help to use the Jewish connection as a kind of chip in getting his parents to explore Mexico. So, the next time they visited him in San Diego, he surprised them by saying he had a hotel reserved for the next night—that French hotel in Ensenada. The next morning he prepared some sandwiches and they took the short drive across the border and then the wonderful if dangerous toll road from Tijuana. It was a beautiful morning, with the sun shining on the bluest of blue waters, sometimes very far down below. Taking a wide curve, they would then see the coastal panorama open up for miles south, and they could even see a few ships cruising down the coast. When they got into town, they checked into the hotel and then strolled the tourist and business streets, until they ate their sandwiches and headed down south out of town toward Estero beach for afternoon

184

margaritas, a walk on the beach and then a visit to the gift store. Then they headed further out along a circular coast out to the Bufadora and spent an hour wandering around on the path which took them to the site where the water crashed against the rocks, sending a dazzling jet of water spraying up from the famous blowhole.

"Jingos," his mother exclaimed, drawing on a word Mel had often heard her use (perhaps a Yiddish evasion of "Jesus") just as a fine mist of water reached her face and hair, "This looks like the world at the end!"

"Well it's as far as I usually go in Ensenada," Mel answered.

Returning to their hotel, they dressed for dinner, and crossed the street for a wonderful French meal at El Rey Sol. His father couldn't resist asking to speak to the owner, a man his own age who spoke to him about the war years and his decision to come to Ensenada, where he had clearly struck it rich. He offered them a fine French pastry and a cognac on the house, told them they shouldn't miss the restaurant's famous Sunday brunch, and suggested what stores to visit (some with Jewish owners) before they left town.

Mel's father, not easily pleased by pretentious restaurants, seemed quite satisfied with his dinner, and his mother virtually glowed from the attentions and the little drink she was offered with the wonderful dessert.

"You know why we got the extras?" Mel's father asked. "It's not because we're Jewish," he continued, "but because I flashed my Masonic ring on him," and he flashed it at Mel as his subtle way of suggesting that his son should stop being such a *jlub,* and get with the Jewish-Masonic conspiracy.

Off they went down the street, where Mel steered them into the night club show of a hotel famous for its folkloric dancers representing different regions of Mexico—a kind of second-rate

185

Ballet Folklórico review, but perfect for his parents who were hardly candidates for Houssong's Saloon serving loud Californians out for a night of heavy drinking, or the strip joints serving the male clientele that arrived especially on the weekends. His parents loved the show and drank their margaritas with pleasure.

It was a long day, and they slept in quite late, waking up in time to walk to the breathtaking fish market, but his mother declined to go along the dock, to see and smell the fish de-headed and carved. Instead, they made it back to the restaurant for brunch just in the nick of time. "That brunch was beyond belief," his mother said upon leaving. "The coffee was just right, the entrees were delicious, and the pastries were to die for."

Again, they wandered around the town checking out some stores the French Jew-friendly Masonic restaurateur had recommended. Only gradually did they make their way back to the car for the trip north.

This time, they took the old road, so his parents could see the countryside between Ensenada and the border, arriving in Tijuana just in time for a light meal at one of the recommended restaurants and then going to the *fronton* only to find it closed for repairs. "Let's try the cockfights," said his father, always game for gambling. So they ended up in a *gallera*, where the music, the noise, the drinks and the betting couldn't compensate for the violence of each combat and the stench of blood and death. It all culminated as one cock blasted his rival and ended up crowing as he picked away at his poor rival's bloody head.

"Let's get out of here," his mother said in a panic. And by the look on her face, they knew they had to move quickly. Out they came, as if tumbling down a funhouse shoot; and a few minutes later, they were in the traffic snarl leading to the border.

"That was awful," she said, sickened to the point of no return. "It was a lovely weekend, but this took the cake right out of my mouth. This is a horrible country, Mel," she said, "You really need to go someplace else. As for me, this is one point I won't return to ever again."

So his parents crossed the border, never to return with Mel, no matter how often he tried to convince them to go. Even after he married again and when he was actually building a life that would send him to Ensenada and other points much further south for the many years that would follow, his parents always declined, pointing to their advancing age and preferring to entertain his new wife and son in their San Fernando Valley apartment.

But some of the better things from those last two border trips must have stuck. Because late in the winter of 1972, after Mel's father had had a serious kidney attack followed by heart complications, he called to tell his son that he and his mom had arranged a synagogue-led cruise from Long Beach to Acapulco with a stop-over in Ensenada and other points south as well as an optional side excursion to Mexico City.

"Dad, do you think you're up for this?"

"Look," his father answered, "The doctors tell me I can live another ten years or die at any minute," he said, "So why shouldn't I go?"

Mel could not argue with that logic—he'd have reasoned in the same way. So he wished his dad well and indeed felt like he might be saying goodbye.

"He's crazy," his mother said when she got on the line, "But there's no way stopping him. I told him I never wanted to go back there, and here we're going for two weeks."

"Just make sure there's a decent doctor on board.," was all he could think to say.

"And you be sure you buy a black tie and shoes, just in case," she answered.

It was indeed the point of no return. Almost two weeks later to the day, Mel received a call from his sister telling him his father had had a heart attack on the love boat, and he should drive up to meet the boat when it docked in Long Beach in the early afternoon. Mel left immediately and then joined his sister and brother-in-law as they boarded the ship and were taken immediately to his parents' cabin. There was their mother, all dressed up and sitting by a casket.

"It was terrible," she told them. "We were dancing cha cha cha one moment, and then we came back to the table, and he said he felt sick. I told the waiter he needed help and before you know it, we were in a sickroom, and he was out like a light. Then the doctor came in and said he was dead right then and there."

At that point she broke down and Mel and his sister patted and consoled her until she regained her composure. "We were right off Ensenada," she exclaimed, almost laughing, right near that nice hotel and restaurant. And I'd said I wouldn't go back and here we were. But they didn't want to make it official. They didn't want to say he died in Mexican waters because if they did, they'd have to delay their departure and we'd have to go through a bunch of paperwork in Spanish and have a big mess with angry passengers at their throats. So, they brought him to the cabin, and we've been together all the way from Ensenada up to here, where they finally pronounced him officially dead just a few minutes ago."

Their talk was interrupted ever so briefly by an official who came in and asked her gently to sign a block of papers. That done, the official told her the casket would be taken to the designated place in the valley, but that she should go with her family. "I'm sorry," his mother told the official. "But I spent the whole night with my husband dead right next to me, and you're not going to separate me from him now."

The official acceded and the family prepared to leave the ship with his mother's luggage and the now useless effects of his father.

"One thing you were right about," his mother said to Mel before entering the hearse, thereby ending one phase, and starting a new one of her life. "We had the time of our lives on this trip. Your father loved every minute, and so did I. Also," she added, "you know, at least he died on the way back instead of on the way out. The point is, he died on the return."

Mel made his way too from the Long Beach pier, and only a few months later, he would say his goodbye to the border, returning from time to time, but really having reached his own point of ... departure.

Chicano Walpurgisnacht

Mel had his first taste of the La Jolla world, when, recently returned from the pre-Olympics turmoil in Mexico 1968, and after a class session he taught at the state university, he went to a rally where a fiery young Chicano student poet he already knew introduced a rather dignified-looking professor—a distinguished but fiery, revolutionary scholar, seemingly taller than his height—Spanish-looking, towering over the poet and the Brown Berets who were there to protect him from Fascists and *halcones*—he denounced police violence and the PRI, responsible for the recent massacre in the Plaza de las tres culturas, speaking out against years of abuse and corruption which were drowning *Mexico querido, lindo pero chingado*. Then it was that the poet came forward, so small on the rostrum that he made the Spanish professor seem all the taller and recited a poem about the Chicano redemption of Mexico, speaking of fire and apocalypse. "Viva la raza!" came the cry.

A year later, Mel's decision to enter graduate school in La Jolla, meant a transition from being professor to being an elder student. The shock of it all was too great and made worse by his sense of starting too late and at a time when he was especially lonely and vulnerable. First, he tried to leave his Mexican and other adventures behind and start a romance with a Romanian Jewish woman who had come to the campus sponsored by a linguistics professor he soon realized was her lover more than her mentor. He was taken with her, but soon understood the limit of their relationship. His all so brief dream of relating to his old-world roots (his mother too was Rumanian Jewish) collapsed; and he began drawing on his limited Mexican experiences to find some sense of relatedness and friendship with those Chicanos, Chicanas, Latinos and Latinas who were fellow-students or professors and who might well become the most intimate context for this new phase of his life.

190

There was beautiful Mirta and her boyfriend Samuel, both from the San Diego barrio; there was Marina Méndez, a tejana, but a graduate like Mel himself from a San Francisco creative writing program. There was a divorcee of 50, half native American/ half Chicana, now starting her graduate studies; there were two rabble-rousing Trotskyist brothers from El Paso studying in La Jolla but teaching and raising hell at the state university, where they both taught and fought for Chicano power as part of the permanent revolution. There was Susana González, a shy, but bright and determined young woman from East L.A. There were Lauro, Clara and Mariana; there was a Chilena, Teresa, with her Korean husband; there was Tina, a Puerto Rican from New York, and next Alberto a Puerto Rican from the island. Then came his professors—one, the son a famous Spanish poet, another, the fiery professor who turned out to be the Mexico City-bred son of Basque exiles and was the husband of the reigning Chicana of their little world; there was Ricardo, a New Mexican literary professor recruited from Dartmouth and straining to be Mr. Chicano radical to please the fiery professor and other hotshots. Then came Amanda, a linguist and feminist more radical (though less Stalinist) than the fiery professor, more feminist than that professor's wife and more Marxist than Marx. And then came a leading Chicano sociologist, an up-and-coming anthropologist, and the Mexican historian who patronized Chicanos and their revolutionary dreams. However, among all these figures, none made an impression on him than a woman from Nicaragua by way of Ensenada, Mexico who would link Mel to things Latin American, Latino and Chicano in more than casual ways for several years to come.

To be sure, Mel's border crossings, his early Chicano barrio theater work and his volunteer picketing of supermarkets in support of UFW boycotts had made him ripe for the concerns that were pushing the campus Latinos; and, now with a new Latina girlfriend, he felt freer to join the campus Latinos as much as they would tacitly

191

allow, in meetings and demonstrations, and almost all the projects they undertook.

Everything crystalized for him when a Chicano labor historian came to campus with an entourage from up north that included a leftwing Jewish American Mexicanist and Chicano studies convert along with his two young Chicano collaborators, Sergio and Alejandra, on one of the first anthologies of Chicano literature. The anthology had just come out and shook up the Latino grad student world, as did the two co-editors, both because of their knowledge and commitment to Chicano art and history but the she of the two also for her compelling allure—especially that dark birthmark on her calf. To cap it off, a brilliant British Latin Americanist came down from Stanford to spend all her spare time with the leftwing Jewish American Mexicanist and Chicano studies convert, and these two leftist critics cooed at every get-together, talked movement talk but always found time for their trip on trip to the racetracks at Aguas Calientes or nearby Del Mar.

The group stayed for weeks, it seemed, meeting with different student organizations, discussing Chicano and Latino struggles nationally and strategizing about local political and cultural struggles as well. Joint meetings were held with Chicanos from San Diego State, the community colleges and even the Latino-heavy high schools. For the first time Mel knew of, meetings were also held with student and artist groups from Tijuana.

Mel got to march in solidarity with Chicano and third world issues; he became the fiery professor's Teaching Assistant and learned more about Mexican and Chicano concerns. He sat in on Latino student meetings that brought Teatro Campesino to be featured performers at a Cinco de Mayo show. The teatro troupe performed their well-known *actos* and answered student questions about the negative portrayals of pachuco zoot-suiters with undocumented workers presented as scabs. A fight raged between the *anti-mojado* UFW Chavistas and the radical Chicanos pushing

192

a *sin fronteras,* without borders internacionalista no-matter-what line. Then things really turned hot when they invited a Tijuana theater group to do a play and the group performed *Los desarraigados,* a work portraying Chicanos as deracinated mexicanos or *pochos* virtually perverted by their *experiencia en gringolandia.* The university crowd tried to remain polite, but things got contentious in the discussion period, with some of the students shouting down their cross-border brothers and sisters for their ideological blindness, their inability to understand what it was to be Chicanao. It all ended with boos, whistles and cries—*chiflas y gritos*—that sent the *tijuanenses* home with their tails between their legs.

Mel joined the Chicanos when they marched in solidarity celebrating the second anniversary of the struggle for Chicano Park and the Centro Cultural de la Raza in Balboa Park. He knew most of the artists and joined their struggle for urban space, justice, and empowerment. He was happy to no longer be considered an outsider looking in, but more or less accepted as one of the regular participants in the demonstrations and of course the fiestas that followed. The biggest one was at the home of the local Chicano poet Mel had known as a student and who was now a cult figure who wrote of fire and spiritual revolution. All the key border area poets and artists showed up, as did grad and undergrad Latino studies students and the visitors from up north, including the alluring anthologist.

In the course of a night which never seemed to end, Susana González dedicated all her time to Sergio, not once seeming to realize that she was barking up the wrong tree; Amanda drifted from room to room seeking Sylvia, Clara and other members of her writing group. Some of the younger women and their profesora conspired with Lauro. The older Chicano Trotskyist brother, Roberto, took up with Mary, Mel's officemate, who fell for him as God's Chicano gift to all Irish Catholic women. It seemed the world became unglued, as the poet intoned Aztlán litanies and couples danced to Santana, while the smell of pot and peyote permeated the crowd. And all the time, the fiery Spanish professor argued with all who were foolish enough to drift from the truth he held so congenially but firmly; his fiery Latina wife presided as queen over the Latino carnival—and all the while, their visiting son from the Sorbonne and Princeton entranced his listeners for hours with as he talked of the Spanish Guerra Civil.

Mel and his new flame were completely into it all, but he made a spectacle of himself when his joking mentor (he who'd evoked the Tlaltleloco massacre) served him up too much tequila añejo so that he was found later spread-eagled on the backyard lawn, barking at the moon and then barfing his guts out as he staggered into the house and finished his show by embracing the toilet as if it were a long lost love. Mary and the Chicano Trotskyist, bonded with Mel and his flame by leaving the party early and taking them home, as he sang revolutionary songs and vomited into a carboard box and then, once in his own bathroom, continued his earlier love affair—though adulterously now, with a new toilet.

What would be the upshot, what identifications and consequences would come to unfold from that night which capped off those Chicano days? In the morning most of the party goers and others left their *crudas* behind and drove in droves down to the border where they formed a giant circle gyrating around the crossing point, with placards of *Sin Fronteras*, *Justicia para los indocumentados*, *Viva la Raza* and *Si se puede*! Chavisitas and internacionalistas, trotskistas, anarquistas y comunistas—those from Tijuana and those from La Jolla—all joined together; performance artists began their skits, as they circled in front of the border and almost in the faces of its guardians (black, white and, yes brown), as they anticipated somehow the Madres de la Plaza de Mayo and the border brujos to come, in the great pre-configuration of nuestra América, Calibán, and Aztlán. So different would the border become in the years to come!

But the days passed by, the visitors returned to points north; Susana never spoke of Sergio again; Mel's office mate and Roberto (he becoming less Trotskyist and more Chicano every day), deepened their relationship—but also their friendship with Mel and his new lady until, once married, she and Mel headed to Europe and then toward the Midwest, to take jobs and make a new start so far from his life in the barrio and, above all, the border which had nurtured him like a second mother, the border to which he now had to say goodbye…

So Many Border Stories

Borders, their crossing, their blockages, their illusions, during his first marriage, in his time between marriages, and in what he more fully and knowingly lived through in the early days of his second. He felt himself regularly confronting multiple borders and orders, always remaining on their edge, never quite violating their boundaries nor knowing which coyotes or border guards might be lying in wait. Some of the most special moments of his life are included and narrated in these stories—mad, sad, or bad as they may be. Some just begged to be told. But there were just too many: and the more he thought about it, the more he remembered.

There are so many stories—so many border anecdotes told here. There are still so many others Mel hasn't yet told and may perhaps never be able to tell before his time and gas run out. Here, we only mention some among those many worthy tales but which he hasn't gotten around to narrating—at least not yet.

There's the story of Alma Orona, lovely in face and smile, black bangs reaching toward her high freckled cheeks and thick lips—Mel falling in love almost at first sight. Always dressed so well, so graceful and intelligent, her father a wayward, heavy drinking mariachi player. She and her mother retreated into an evangelical church, even as Alma gave dancing lessons for Fred Astaire Studios. Though she walked hand in hand with Mel at a municipal fiesta in Tijuana's Parque Libertad, she resisted his every insinuation and every effort to kiss her and declare his feelings, explaining that, for religious and cultural reasons, she could not form a deeper relation with him. She never dated him again. Mel, though, would see her one more time during his second marriage, this time walking down the street in Madrid's Plaza del Sol, holding hands with a flashy young Spaniard who didn't have the look of an evangelical preacher.

There was that evening when after several years, when Mel's old, almost lost friend Bob, his first teacher of Spanish, came to visit after a meeting he'd gone to in San Diego, and they then crossed the border together for the first time since their trip in 1960, hitting several hooker bars, flirting with bar girls and prostitutes, but choosing finally to recross the border to eat breakfast at the Denny's in National City.

There was the day during the first terrible month of his entrance into graduate school, when, torn by loneliness and the fear of his possibly never being able to get through the doctoral program, he received a letter offering him a job at a community college on the border. He called his parents to tell them the fine news. "I'll have a fine salary and be able to cross the border to explore Mexico whenever I want." It was his mother who said, "But you'd drop all your ambitions to reach the peak of your profession and choose to live a simple, almost anonymous border life?" He knew she had a point once again, and decided not to travel down that road, even though it might turn out to mean what in fact it turned out to mean— that he would eventually have to leave the border after all.

And there was the day when a Latina student from Ensenada spoke up to counter what he put forth in an English class he was teaching, and that began a new period of border life and far richer stories—his time of Nicaraguan stories on the border. when Mel became fully involved in the struggle against Somoza as it played itself out on the border (but those stories won't be told here).

There were times when friends from La Jolla visited Mel and his then new wife at her mother's home in Ensenada, or when they'd go with friends to Tijuana, to buy radical Spanish language books at La Librería El Día. They'd go for lunch at the Basque restaurant on Avenida Revolución or eat tacos in that cellar restaurant a few blocks down the street, or at Carnitas Uruápan on yet another street.

There was a time when one of the couple's friends, Susana González, crossed over with them for the day. On the way back, she felt so put upon that when, staring at her driver's license the border guard, asked where she was from. She said (was it a simple reflex or a prideful assertion?) a simple *Los Ángeles*, with a Spanish accent—and with the result that everyone in the car was held up.

There were days when he saw whole busloads of *mexicanos* passing on the freeway as part a caravan of buses (legal or just openly illegal) from across the border to do the low paid farm work farm owners required to deliver the low-cost farm products Californians and other consumers desired. There was more than one time at the San Onofre checkpoint on the way to L.A. when he saw *mexicanos* hauled out of a car trunk and retained by some tough border guards and once when he saw a guy leap out of a truck and dodge traffic as he tried to avoid the *migra* (but he didn't make it).

There were later times when his third wife (not the Ensenada nicaragüense) shocked Valenzuela Arce, their oh so knowing border guide, by pointing out the fine handicraft all but hidden among the schlock on Avenida Revolución, even finding a brilliant paper maché artist, El Cordobés, who made magnificent *muertos* figures comparable to the best from Oaxaca. They spent the rest of a day searching for him, but the wary shopkeepers kept his identity and whereabouts unknown. Just one more border mystery on top of so many others.

Then there was the time Valenzuela Arce invited him to a conference at el Colegio de la frontera; and he, his third wife and friends made their way to Ensenada on a scorching day, walking through the grand fish market now stinking from the heat, touring the amazing new wineries in the Valle de Guadalupe and even landed in Tecate and, yes, the Diana Bar, seeing the huge nude statue of the maiden hunter goddess (more voluptuous Afrodite than chaste Artemis) all but dominating the scene.

So many other border stories; so many encounters with so many different people of all kinds—*payasos y pendejos, cabrones, coyotes, and come-mierdas*, wisemen, and fools . . . So many people, so many women caught in the lives they were forced to live—so many tragedies and comedies, until the day came when, graduate school behind him, the job market would take him from the border to which he would return several times, but where he would never live again.

His life on the border had had endless dimensions. While his trips into Mexico were often touristy and repetitious (those seemingly endless roads, those women he would try to meet), they were the beginning of all he would learn beyond the border. Of these deeper Mexican things, he could only impart some few aspects here, hoping the stories told would stand for so much more. He could only hope that what he could tell would illuminate and memorialize those people he knew and many he never was to know at all. He could only hope always to be able to cross all a depth of knowledge about his initial selves, his subsequent ones—and yes, more and more, the selves of others he might never have otherwise come to know.

There were other, later border visits, other stories but they won't be mentioned here. The most important stories would be the wave of Central American kids (so many lost boys and girls) on the border—the Honduran caravans, La Bestia, the detention centers, the separation of families, the continued hate talk about building a wall. How would all this play out on the Tijuana and San Diego sides of it all? But these would not be stories he could tell well, for he was by then just an almost old man seeking to relive an older border world that was deep inside him but was no longer the same and was no longer, if it had ever at all been, his.

ABOUT MARC ZIMMERMAN

Marc Zimmerman is Professor Emeritus of Latin American and Latino Studies at the University of Illinois in Chicago (UIC) as well as World Cultures and Literatures and Hispanic Studies at the University of Houston, where he served as chair (2002-2008), involving considerable work with Latin American Studies programs. Zimmerman served in Nicaragua's Ministerio de Cultura during the first year of the Sandinista Revolution. He has been director of Global CASA/ LACASA Books since 1998; and he has written and edited over forty books on world, Latin American and Latino cultural and literary studies. He has won Fulbright, Rockefeller, Puerto Rican Studies and other major awards; he has served on the jury of Cuba's Casa de la Américas, and been guest professor at McGill U., the Universidades de Madrid, Puerto Rico, Nicaragua, and Tucumán, Argentina.

While Zimmerman holds a Ph.D. in Comparative Literature from the U. of California San Diego, he also holds an M.A. in Creative Writing from San Francisco State U., where he studied with Walter Van Tilburg Clark, Herbert Blau, Mark Harris, Marvin Halperin, James Scheville, Ray West, and Herbert Wilner. His early stories were published in *The Dartmouth Quarterly*, *Descant*, *The Great River Review*, and (in translation) *Nuova Prosa*, a key fiction journal in Milan, Italy. More recent stories have appeared in the Chicago Latino online journal, *El BeiSMan*, as well as in *Voices in Italian Americana* and *Literal*, a Latin American literary journal.

Recently, Zimmerman has completed a new book early Chicago Mexican and Chicano writing (2023); and he has coordinated the development of a series of interviews and related materials entitled "The Chicago Latino Artist Series Project (CLASP)," which he donated to the Smithsonian American Art

History Collection. Based on this ongoing work, Zimmerman has thus far published books and CDs centered on Chicago Mexican artists José Gamaliel González (2010 and 2013), Aaron Kerlow (2015) and José Guerrero (2016); he has presented and published work on Chicago Central American and Puerto Rican art, as he develops a book based on his Chicago Latino art research.

Returning to his first love of creative writing, Zimmerman has also been developing a book series of books of "autofiction" (related life-based stories, dreams and fantasies organized into novel-like structures), *Illusions of Memory* touching on Jewish, Italian, African and Central American, but above all Mexican/Chicano, Central American and Puerto Rican themes— with eleven books published and several others in progress, and with four volumes translated into Spanish and one into Italian.

In recent years, Zimmerman has lectured on Chicago Latino art at Dartmouth College, the U. of California Berkeley and San Diego, Purdue U., and the Universidad de Costa Rica. He has read from his fiction in Italy at Milano's Verso Bookstore and the Torino International Book Fair, in California at the University Press Book Store in Berkeley, the Tía Chucha Cultural Center and Pop-Hop Books in the L.A. area, the Media Center in San Diego, the Avid Reader in Davis, and the Green Arcade in San Francisco—as well as in public libraries in East Los Angeles and La Jolla. In Chicago, he has read for the Palabra Pura program of the Guild Complex, the Heirloom Bookstore, and the Lozano Public Library. In Puerto Rico, he has read at Librería Laberinto in San Juan and Librería Candil in Ponce, as well as in a seminar at El Centro de Estudios Avanzados in El Viejo San Juan. For additional presentations, he may be reached at tel. (281) 513-9475 or mzimmerman@uh.edu. To visit his author's website and above all his Illusions of Memory series, visir www.marczimmerman.net.

He and his wife Esther Soler from Quebradillas, Puerto Rico, divide each year between the island and the Wicker Park/ Humboldt Park area of Chicago. They continue to travel each year to Minnesota and California—to Mexico, Europe, and wherever else they can.

Books in Marc Zimmerman's Autofiction series, Illusions of Memory

(Ordered in relation to the author's life history)[1]

A. Overviews, 1939—

The Short of it All—1945-2016
Stores of Winter—1945-1960s
The Italian Daze—1950s-2016
     Italian Version: La penisola non trovata
A Mexican Maze Without Borders —1979-2021

Forthcoming:

Black Matters and Byways—1950-2022
Jewish American Days—1939-
Latin American Ways—1969-
The Puerto Rican Phase—1981-

B.   Cycle I. 1939-1979-80

Seeds of Becoming—1939-1961
No Light from Heaven—1961-1966
Black, Brown and White on the Border—1967-1972
Nicas on the Border—1969—
Managua, Mon Amour (Nevermore)—1969-1980 and beyond.

C.   Cycle II. 1979— LACASA

Martín and Melvin—1981-2005

Forthcoming (Tentative Projection):

In the Jungle of the City—1981-1988

---

[1] Visit www. marczimmerman.net for details on all these books, plus other books and editions by Zimmerman.

A Professor and Wife in Chicago—1988-2001
Hot Houston Times—2001-2010
The Final Years—2010-?

Books in Spanish:

Cuán alta la luna
Amores fronterizos
Sandino en la frontera
Martín y Marvin